What Is Populism?

What Is Populism?

Jan-Werner Müller

PENN

UNIVERSITY OF PENNSYLVANIA PRESS

PHILADELPHIA

Published by
University of Pennsylvania Press
Philadelphia, Pennsylvania 19104-4112
www.upenn.edu/pennpress

Printed in the United States of America

A Cataloging-in-Publication record is available from the Library of Congress

Cover design by Bradford Foltz

ISBN 978-0-8122-4898-2 hardcover
ISBN 978-0-8122-9378-4 e-book

The only meaning I can see in the word "people" is "mixture"; if you substitute for the word "people" the words "number" and "mixture," you will get some very odd terms . . . "the sovereign mixture," "the will of the mixture," etc.

—Paul Valéry

All power comes from the people. But where does it go?

—Bertolt Brecht

Contents

Is Everyone a Populist?

No US election campaign in living memory has seen as many invocations of "populism" as the one unfolding in 2015–16. Both Donald Trump and Bernie Sanders have been labelled "populists." The term is regularly used as a synonym for "antiestablishment," irrespective, it seems, of any particular political ideas; content, as opposed to attitude, simply doesn't seem to matter. The term is thus also primarily associated with particular moods and emotions: populists are "angry"; their voters are "frustrated" or suffer from "resentment." Similar claims are made about political leaders in Europe and their followers: Marine Le Pen and Geert Wilders, for instance, are commonly referred to as populists. Both these politicians are clearly on the right. But, as with the Sanders phenomenon, left-wing insurgents are also labeled populists: there is Syriza in Greece, a left-wing alliance that came to power in January 2015, and Podemos in Spain, which shares with Syriza a fundamental opposition to Angela Merkel's austerity policies in response to the Eurocrisis. Both—especially Podemos—make a point of feeling inspired by what is commonly referred to as the "pink tide" in Latin America: the success of populist leaders such as Rafael Correa, Evo Morales, and, above all, Hugo Chávez. Yet what do all these political actors actually have in common? If we hold with Hannah Arendt that political judgment is the capacity to draw proper distinctions, the widespread conflation of right and left when talking about populism should give us pause. Might the popularity of diagnosing all kinds of different phenomena as "populism" be a failure of political judgment?

This book starts with the observation that, for all the talk about populism—the Bulgarian political scientist Ivan Krastev, one of the sharpest analysts of democratic life today, has even called our time an "Age of Populism"—it is far from obvious that we know what we are talking about.[1] We simply do not have anything like a *theory* of populism, and we seem to lack coherent criteria for deciding when political actors turn populist in some meaningful sense. After all, every politician—especially in poll-driven democracies—wants to appeal to "the people," all want to tell a story that can be understood by as many citizens as possible, all want to be sensitive to how "ordinary folks" think and, in particular, feel. Might a populist simply be a successful politician one doesn't like? Can the charge "populism" perhaps itself be populist? Or might, in the end, populism actually be "the authentic voice of democracy," as Christopher Lasch maintained?

This book seeks to help us recognize and deal with populism. It aims to do so in three ways. First, I want to give an account of what kind of political actor qualifies as populist. I argue that it is a necessary but not sufficient condition to be *critical of elites* in order to count as a populist. Otherwise, anyone criticizing the status quo in, for instance, Greece, Italy, or the United States would by definition be a populist—and, whatever else one thinks about Syriza, Beppe Grillo's insurgent Five Star Movement, or Sanders, for that matter, it's hard to deny that their attacks on elites can often be justified. Also, virtually every presidential candidate in the United States would be a populist, if criticism of existing elites is all there is to populism: everyone, after all, runs "against Washington."

In addition to being antielitist, populists are always *antipluralist*. Populists claim that they, and they alone, represent the people. Think, for instance, of Turkish President Recep Tayyip Erdoğan declaring at a party congress in defiance of his numerous domestic critics, "We are the people. Who are you?" Of course, he knew that his opponents were Turks, too. The claim to exclusive representation is not an empirical one; it is always distinctly *moral*. When running for office, populists portray their political competitors as part of the immoral, corrupt elite; when ruling, they refuse to recognize any opposition as legitimate. The populist logic also implies that whoever does not support populist parties might not be a proper part of the people—always defined as righteous and morally pure. Put simply, populists do not claim "We are the 99 percent." What they imply instead is "We are the 100 percent."

For populists, this equation always works out: any remainder can be dismissed as immoral and not properly a part of the people at all. That's another way of saying that populism is always *a form of identity politics* (though not all versions of identity politics are populist). What follows from this understanding of populism as an exclusionary form of identity politics is that populism tends to pose a danger to democracy. For democracy requires pluralism and the recognition that we need to find fair terms of living together as free, equal, but also irreducibly diverse citizens. The idea of the single, homogeneous, authentic people is a fantasy; as the philosopher Jürgen Habermas once put it, "the people" can only appear in the plural. And it's a dangerous fantasy, because populists do not just thrive on conflict and encourage polarization; they also treat their political opponents as "enemies of the people" and seek to exclude them altogether.

This is not to say that all populists will send their enemies to a gulag or build walls along the country's borders, but neither is populism limited to harmless campaign rhetoric or a mere protest that burns out as soon as a populist wins power. Populists can govern as populists. This goes against the conventional wisdom, which holds that populist protest parties cancel themselves out once they win an election, since by definition one cannot protest against oneself in government. Populist governance exhibits three features: attempts to hijack the state apparatus, corruption and "mass clientelism" (trading material benefits or bureaucratic favors for political support by citizens who become the populists' "clients"), and efforts systematically to suppress civil society. Of course, many authoritarians will do similar things. The difference is that populists justify their conduct by claiming that they alone represent the people; this allows populists to avow their practices quite openly. It also explains why revelations of corruption rarely seem to hurt populist leaders (think of Erdoğan in Turkey or the far-right populist Jörg Haider in Austria). In the eyes of their followers, "they're doing it for us," the one authentic people. The second chapter of this volume shows how populists will even write constitutions (with Venezuela and Hungary serving as the most clear-cut examples). Contrary to the image of populist leaders preferring to be entirely unconstrained by relying on disorganized masses that they directly address from the balcony of a presidential palace, populists in fact often want to create constraints, so long as they function in an entirely partisan fashion. Rather than serving as instruments to preserve pluralism, here constitutions serve to eliminate it.

The third chapter addresses some of the deeper causes of populism, in particular recent socioeconomic developments across the West. It also raises the question of how one can successfully respond to both populist politicians and their voters. I reject the paternalistic liberal attitude that effectively prescribes therapy for citizens "whose fears and anger have to be taken seriously" as well as the notion that mainstream actors should simply copy populist proposals. Neither is the other extreme of excluding populists from debate altogether a viable option, since it simply responds to the populist will to exclusion by excluding the populist. As an alternative, I suggest some specific political terms of how to confront populists.

More than a quarter of a century ago, a virtually unknown State Department official published a notorious and widely misunderstood article. The author was Francis Fukuyama and the title was, of course, "The End of History." It has long been a lazy way to establish one's intellectual sophistication to say with a sneer that obviously history did not end with the conclusion of the Cold War. But of course, Fukuyama had not predicted the end of all conflict. He had simply wagered that there were no more rivals to liberal democracy at the level of ideas. He conceded that here and there, other ideologies might enjoy support, but he nonetheless maintained that none of them would be capable of competing with liberal democracy's (and market capitalism's) global attractiveness.

Was he so obviously wrong? Radical Islamism is no serious ideological threat to liberalism. (Those who conjure up the specter of "Islamofascism" tell us more about their longing for clear-cut battle lines comparable to those that prevailed during the Cold War than they do about the political realities of the present.) What is now sometimes called "the China model" of state-controlled capitalism obviously inspires some as a new model of meritocracy, and perhaps none more so than those who consider themselves as having the greatest merit.[2] (Think Silicon Valley entrepreneurs.) It also inspires through its track record of lifting millions out of poverty—especially, but not only, in developing countries. Yet "democracy" remains the chief political prize, with authoritarian governments paying lobbyists and public relations experts enormous sums of money to ensure that they, too, are recognized by international organizations and Western elites as genuine democracies.

Yet all is not well for democracy. The danger to democracies today is not some comprehensive ideology that systematically denies democratic ideals. The danger is populism—a degraded form of democracy that promises to make good on democracy's highest ideals ("Let the people rule!"). The danger comes, in other words, from within the democratic world—the political actors posing the danger speak the language of democratic values. That the end result is a form of politics that is blatantly antidemocratic should trouble us all—and demonstrate the need for nuanced political judgment to help us determine precisely where democracy ends and populist peril begins.

What Populists Say

"A spectre is haunting the world: populism."[1] Thus wrote Ghita Ionescu and Ernest Gellner in the introduction to an edited volume on populism published in 1969. The book was based on papers delivered at a very large conference held at the London School of Economics in 1967, with the aim "to define populism." The many participants, it turned out, could not agree on such a definition. Yet reading the proceedings of the gathering can still be instructive. One cannot help thinking that then, just as today, all kinds of political anxieties get articulated in talk about "populism"—with the word *populism* being used for many political phenomena that appear at first sight to be mutually exclusive. Given that today we also don't seem to be able to agree on a definition, one might be tempted to ask, Is there a there there?

Back in the late 1960s, "populism" appeared in debates about decolonization, speculations concerning the future of "peasantism," and, perhaps most surprising from our vantage point at the beginning of the twenty-first century, discussions about the origins and likely developments of Communism in general and Maoism in particular. Today, especially in Europe, all kinds of anxieties—and, much less often, hopes—also crystallize around the word *populism*. Put schematically, on the one hand, liberals seem to be worried about what they see as increasingly illiberal masses falling prey to populism, nationalism, and even outright xenophobia; theorists of democracy, on the other hand, are concerned about the rise of what they see as "liberal technocracy"—which is to say, "responsible governance" by an elite of experts that is consciously not responsive to the wishes of ordinary citizens.[2] Populism might then be what the Dutch social scientist Cas Mudde has called an "illiberal democratic response to undemocratic liberalism." Populism is seen as a threat but also as a potential corrective for a politics that has somehow become too distant from "the people."[3] There might be something to the striking image Benjamin Arditi has proposed to capture the relationship between populism and democracy. Populism, according to Arditi, resembles a drunken guest at a dinner party: he's not respecting table manners, he is rude, he might even start "flirting with the wives of other guests." But he might also be blurting out the truth about a liberal democracy that has become forgetful about its founding ideal of popular sovereignty.[4]

In the United States, the word *populism* remains mostly associated with the idea of a genuine *egalitarian* left-wing politics in potential conflict with the stances of a Democratic Party that, in the eyes of populist critics, has become too centrist or, echoing the discussion in Europe, has been captured by and for technocrats (or, even worse, "plutocrats"). After all, it is in particular the defenders of "Main Street" against "Wall Street" who are lauded (or loathed) as populists. This is the case even when they are established politicians, such as New York

City mayor Bill de Blasio and Massachusetts senator Elizabeth Warren. In the United States, it is common to hear people speak of "liberal populism," whereas that expression in Europe would be a blatant contradiction, given the different understandings of *both* liberalism and populism on the two sides of the Atlantic.[5] As is well known, "liberal" means something like "Social Democratic" in North America, and "populism" suggests an uncompromising version of it; in Europe, by contrast, populism can never be combined with liberalism, if one means by the latter something like a respect for pluralism and an understanding of democracy as necessarily involving checks and balances (and, in general, constraints on the popular will).

As if these different political usages of the same word were not already confusing enough, matters have been further complicated by the rise of new movements in the wake of the financial crisis, in particular the Tea Party and Occupy Wall Street. Both have variously been described as populist, to the extent that even a coalition between right-wing and left-wing forces critical of mainstream politics has been suggested, with "populism" as the potential common denominator. This curious sense of symmetry has only been reinforced by the ways in which the 2016 presidential contest has widely been described in the media: Donald Trump and Bernie Sanders are supposedly both populists, with one on the right and the other one on the left. Both, we are frequently told, have at least in common that they are "antiestablishment insurgents" propelled by the "anger," "frustration," or "resentment" of citizens.

Populism is obviously a politically contested concept.[6] Professional politicians themselves know the stakes of the battle over its meaning. In Europe, for instance, ostensible "establishment figures" are eager to tag their opponents as populists. But some of those labeled as populists have gone on the counterattack. They have proudly claimed the label for themselves with the argument that, if populism means working for the people, then they are indeed populists. How are we to judge such claims, and how should we draw distinctions between real populists and those who are merely branded as populists (and perhaps others who are never called populists, never call themselves populists, and yet still might be populists)? Are we not facing complete conceptual chaos, as almost anything—left, right, democratic, antidemocratic, liberal, illiberal—can be called populist, and populism can be viewed as both friend and foe of democracy?

How to proceed, then? In this chapter, I take three steps. First, I try to show why several common approaches to understanding populism in fact lead down dead ends: a social-psychological perspective focused on voters' feelings; a sociological analysis fixated on certain classes; and an assessment of the quality of policy proposals can all be somewhat helpful in understanding populism, but they do not properly delineate what populism is and how it might differ from other phenomena. (Nor is it helpful to listen to the self-descriptions of political actors, as if one automatically becomes a populist simply by using the term.) In place of these approaches, I will follow a different path to understanding populism.[7]

Populism, I argue, is not anything like a codified doctrine, but it is a set of distinct claims and has what one might call an inner logic. When that logic is examined, one discovers that populism is not a useful corrective for a democracy that somehow has come to be too "elite-driven," as many observers hold. The image according to which liberal democracy involves a balance where we can choose to have a little bit more liberalism or a little bit more democracy is fundamentally misleading. To be sure, democracies can legitimately differ on questions such as the possibility and frequency of referenda or the power of judges to invalidate laws overwhelmingly passed in a legislature. But the notion that we move closer to democracy by pitting a "silent majority," which supposedly is being ignored by elites, against elected politician is not just an illusion; it is a politically pernicious thought. In that sense, I believe that a proper grasp of populism also helps deepen our understanding of democracy. Populism is something like a permanent shadow of modern representative democracy, and a constant peril. Becoming aware of its character can help us see the distinctive features—and, to some degree, also the shortcomings—of the democracies we actually live in.[8]

Understanding Populism: Dead Ends

The notion of populism as somehow "progressive" or "grassroots" is largely an American (North, Central, and South) phenomenon. In Europe, one finds a different historically conditioned preconception of populism. There populism is connected, primarily by liberal commentators, with irresponsible policies or various forms of political pandering ("demagoguery" and "populism" are often used interchangeably). As Ralf Dahrendorf once put it, populism is simple; democracy is complex.[9] More particularly, there is a long-standing association of "populism" with the accumulation of public debt—an association that has also dominated recent discussions of parties like Syriza in Greece and Podemos in Spain, which are classified by many European commentators as instances of "left-wing populism."

Populism is also frequently identified with a particular class, especially the petty bourgeoisie and, until peasants and farmers disappeared from the European and the American political imaginations (ca. 1979, I'd say), those engaged in cultivating the land. This can seem like a sociologically robust theory (classes are constructs, of course, but they can be empirically specified in fairly precise ways). This approach usually comes with an additional set of criteria drawn from social psychology: those espousing populist claims publicly and, in particular, those casting ballots for populist parties, are said to be driven by "fears" (of modernization, globalization, etc.) or feelings of "anger," "frustration," and "resentment."

Finally, there is a tendency among historians and social scientists—in both Europe and the United States—to say that populism is best specified by examining what parties and movements that at some point in the past have called themselves "populists" have in common. One can then read the relevant features of the "-ism" in question off the self-descriptions of the relevant historical actors.

In my view, none of these perspectives or seemingly straightforward empirical criteria is helpful for conceptualizing populism. Given how widespread these perspectives are—and how often seemingly empirical and neutral diagnoses such as "lower-middle class" and "resentment" are deployed without much thinking—I want to spell out my objections in some detail.

First of all, when examining the quality of policies, it's hard to deny that some policies justified with reference to "the people" really can turn out to have been irresponsible: those deciding on such policies did not think hard enough; they failed to gather all the relevant evidence; or, most plausibly, their knowledge of the likely long-term consequences should have made them refrain from policies with only short-term electoral benefits for themselves. One does not have to be a neoliberal technocrat to judge some policies as plainly irrational. Think of Hugo Chávez's hapless successor as president of Venezuela, Nicolás Maduro, who sought to fight inflation by sending soldiers into electronics stores and having them put stickers with lower prices on products. (Maduro's preferred theory of inflation came down to "parasites of the bourgeoisie" as the main cause.) Or think of the French Front National, which in the 1970s and 1980s put up posters saying "Two Million Unemployed Is Two Million Immigrants Too Many!" The equation was so simple that everyone could solve it and seemingly figure out with *bon sens* what the correct policy solution had to be.

Still, we cannot generate a criterion for what constitutes populism this way. For in most areas of public life, there simply is no absolutely clear, uncontested line between responsibility and irresponsibility. Often enough, charges of irresponsibility are themselves highly partisan (and the irresponsible policies most frequently denounced almost always benefit the worst-off).[10] In any case, making a political debate a matter of "responsible" versus "irresponsible" poses the question, Responsible according to which values or larger commitments?[11] Free trade agreements—to take an obvious example—can be responsible in light of a commitment to maximizing overall GDP and yet have distributional consequences that one might find unacceptable in light of other values. The debate then has to be about the value commitments of a society as a whole, or perhaps about the different income distributions that follows from different economic theories. Setting up a distinction between populism and responsible policies only obscures the real issues at stake. It can also be an all-too-convenient way to discredit criticism of certain policies.

Focusing on particular socioeconomic groups as the main supporters of populism is no less misleading. It is also empirically dubious, as a number of studies have shown.[12] Less obviously, such an argument often results from a largely discredited set of assumptions from modernization theory. It is true that in many cases, voters who support what might initially be called populist parties share a certain income and educational profile: especially in Europe, those who vote for what are commonly referred to as right-wing populist parties make less and are less educated. (They are also overwhelmingly male—a finding that holds for the United States as well, but not for Latin America.)[13] Yet this picture is by no means always true. As the German social scientist Karin Priester has shown, economically successful citizens often adopt an essentially Social Darwinist attitude and justify their support for right-wing parties by asking, in effect, "I have made it—why can't they?" (Think of the Tea Party placard demanding "Redistribute My Work Ethic!")[14] Not least, in some countries such as France and Austria, populist parties have become so large that they effectively resemble what used to be called "catch-all parties": they attract a large number of workers, but their voters also come from many other walks of life.

A number of surveys have shown that one's personal socioeconomic situation and support for right-wing populist parties often do not correlate at all, because the latter is based on a much more general assessment of the situation of one's country.[15] It would be misleading to reduce perceptions of national decline or danger ("Elites are robbing us of our own country!") to personal fears or "status anxiety." Many supporters of populist parties actually pride themselves on doing their own thinking (even their own research) about the political situation and deny that their stances are just about them or are driven merely by emotions.[16]

One should be very careful indeed about using such loaded terms as "frustration," "anger," and especially "resentment" to explain populism. There are at least two reasons for this. First, while commentators invoking a term like *resentment* might not be rehearsing Nietzsche's *The Genealogy of Morality* in the back of their minds, it is hard to see how one could entirely avoid certain connotations of *ressentiment*. Those suffering from resentment are by definition weak, even if in Nietzsche's analysis those consumed by resentment can become creative, with the cleverest among the weak vanquishing the strong by reordering the rank of human values. The resentful are nonetheless defined by their inferiority and their *reactive* character.[17] They feel bad about the strong and bottle up that feeling; their self-understanding is thus fundamentally dependent on the strong, as they ultimately long for proper recognition by the superior. In that sense, the resentful are always incapable of anything like autonomous conduct. They have to keep lying to themselves about their own actual condition, even if they can never quite believe their own lies. As Max Scheler put it, resentment leads humans slowly to poison their own souls.[18]

Now, maybe one really believes that this is actually true of all people who wear baseball caps emblazoned with the slogan "Make America Great Again." Or that those who vote for populist parties always have authoritarian personalities or perhaps what social psychologists call "low agreeable personalities."[19] But one should at least face up to the political consequences of such psychologizing diagnoses—namely, that they end up confirming those people's view of "liberal elites" as being not just deeply condescending but also constitutively unable to live up to their own democratic ideals by failing to take ordinary people at their word, preferring instead to prescribe political therapy as a cure for fearful and resentful citizens. The simple fact is that "anger" and "frustration" might not always be very articulate—but they are also not "just emotions" in the sense of being completely divorced from thought. There are *reasons* for anger and frustration, which most people can actually spell out in some form or other.[20] This is not to say, of course, that all these reasons are plausible and should just be accepted at face value; the feeling of having been wronged or sentiments that "the country has been taken away from us" are certainly not self-validating. But simply to shift the discussion to social psychology (and treat the angry and frustrated as potential patients for a political sanatorium) is to neglect a basic democratic duty to engage in reasoning. Here seemingly enlightened liberals appear to be repeating the very exclusionary gestures of some of their illustrious nineteenth-century predecessors who were wary of extending the franchise because the masses were "too emotional" to exercise the vote responsibly.

Now, even if one were to conclude that nothing should prevent elites from criticizing the value commitments of ordinary citizens, it is still rather peculiar to conflate the content of a set of political beliefs with the socioeconomic positions and the psychological states of its supporters. This is like saying that the best way to understand Social Democracy is to redescribe its voters as workers envious of rich people. The profile of supporters of populism obviously matters in how we think about the phenomenon. But it is not just patronizing to explain the entire phenomenon as an inarticulate political expression on the part of the supposed "losers in the process of modernization." It is also not really an explanation.

Then why do so many of us keep resorting to it? Because consciously or unconsciously, we continue to draw on a set of assumptions derived from modernization theory that had its heyday in the 1950s and 1960s. This is true even of many political theorists and social scientists who, if asked, would say they consider modernization theory to be thoroughly discredited. It was liberal intellectuals like Daniel Bell, Edward Shils, and Seymour Martin Lipset (all heirs of Max Weber) who in the course of the 1950s began to describe what they considered to be "populism" as a helpless articulation of anxieties and anger by those longing for a simpler, "premodern" life.[21] Lipset, for instance, claimed that populism was attractive for "the disgruntled and the psychologically homeless, . . . the personal failures, the socially isolated, the economically insecure, the uneducated, unsophisticated, and authoritarian personalities."[22] The immediate targets of these social theorists were McCarthyism and the John Birch

Society—but their diagnosis often extended to the original American populist revolt of the late nineteenth century. Victor C. Ferkiss, for instance, saw the followers of the Farmer's Alliance and the People's Party as nothing less than the precursors of a distinct American variety of fascism.[23] This thesis was not to remain uncontested—but the background assumptions are still present among many social and political commentators today.[24]

Finally, there is the thought that populism must have something to do with those who first called themselves populists. Think of the Russian *narodniki* in the late nineteenth century and their ideology of *Narodnichestvo*, which is usually translated as "populism." The *narodniki* were intellectuals who idealized the Russian peasants and saw the village commune as a political model for the country as a whole. They also advocated "going to the people" for political advice and guidance. (Like many urban intellectuals, they found that "the people" neither welcomed them in the ways they had hoped nor recognized the political prescriptions deduced from their supposedly "pure ways of life" by intellectuals.)

For many observers, there simply has to be a reason something called "populism" emerged simultaneously in Russia and the United States toward the end of the nineteenth century. The fact that both movements had something to do with farmers and peasants gave rise to the notion—prevalent at least until the 1970s—that populism had a close connection to agrarianism or that it was necessarily a revolt of reactionary, economically backward groups in rapidly modernizing societies.

While that association is largely lost today, the origins of "populism" in the United States in particular still suggests to many observers that populism must at least on some level be "popular" in the sense of favoring the least advantaged or bringing the excluded into politics—a sense that is reinforced by a glance at Latin America, where the advocates of populism have always stressed its inclusionary and emancipatory character in what remains the most economically unequal continent on the globe.

To be sure, one cannot simply by fiat ban such associations: historical languages are what they are and, as Nietzsche taught us, only that which has no history can be defined. But political and social theory also cannot simply root itself in one particular historical experience— with, for example, every form of populism presumed to fit the template of the American People's Party.[25] We have to allow for the possibility that a plausible understanding of populism will in fact end up excluding historical movements and actors who explicitly called themselves populists. With very few exceptions, historians (or political theorists, to the extent that they care about such historical phenomena) would not argue that a proper understanding of socialism needs to make room for National Socialism just because the Nazis called themselves socialists. But then, to decide which historical experience really fits a particular "-ism," we must of course have a theory of that particular "-ism." So what is populism?

The Logic of Populism

Populism, I suggest, is a particular *moralistic imagination of politics*, a way of perceiving the political world that sets a morally pure and fully unified—but, I shall argue, ultimately fictional—people against elites who are deemed corrupt or in some other way morally inferior.[26] It is a necessary but not a sufficient condition to be critical of elites in order to qualify as a populist. Otherwise, anyone criticizing the powerful and the status quo in any country would by definition be a populist. In addition to being antielitist, populists are always antipluralist: populists claim that they, *and only they*, represent the people.[27] Other political competitors are just part of the immoral, corrupt elite, or so populists say, while not having power themselves; when in government, they will not recognize anything like a legitimate opposition. The populist core claim also implies that whoever does not really support populist parties might not be part of the proper people to begin with. In the words of the French philosopher Claude Lefort, the supposedly real people first has to be "extracted" from the sum total of actual citizens.[28] This ideal people is then presumed to be morally pure and unerring in its will.

Populism arises with the introduction of representative democracy; it is its shadow. Populists hanker after what the political theorist Nancy Rosenblum has called "holism": the notion that the polity should no longer be split and the idea that it's possible for the people to be one and—all of them—to have one true representative.[29] The core claim of populism is thus a moralized form of antipluralism. Political actors not committed to this claim are simply not populists.[30] Populism requires a *pars pro toto* argument and a claim to exclusive representation, with both understood in a moral, as opposed to empirical, sense.[31] There can be no populism, in other words, without someone speaking in the name of the people as a whole.

Think of George Wallace's infamous statement upon his inauguration as governor of Alabama: "In the name of the greatest people that have ever trod this earth, I draw the line in the dust and toss the gauntlet before the feet of tyranny . . . and I say . . . segregation now . . . segregation tomorrow . . . segregation forever."[32] Segregation did not last forever, but what Wallace said about it tarnished his reputation forever; it was clearly racism. Yet the rhetoric that revealed Wallace to be a populist centered on his claim exclusively to speak "in the name of the greatest people that have ever trod this earth." What exactly gave the governor of Alabama the right to speak in the name of all Americans—minus, evidently, the proponents of "tyranny," which meant, of course, the Kennedy administration and everyone else who was working to end segregation? And what allowed him, furthermore, to claim that the "real America" was what he called "the Great Anglo-Saxon Southland"?[33] Clearly, everything good and authentic in the United States was Southern, or so it seemed when Wallace exclaimed, "And you native sons and daughters of old New England's rock-ribbed patriotism . . . and you sturdy natives of the great mid-West . . . and you descendants of the far West flaming spirit of pioneer freedom . . . we invite you to come and be with us . . . for you are of the Southern mind . . . and the Southern spirit . . . and the Southern philosophy . . . you are Southerners too and brothers with us in our fight." Toward the end of the address, Wallace claimed that virtually all Founding Fathers had been Southerners.[34]

This is the core claim of populism: only some of the people are really the people. Think of Nigel Farage celebrating the Brexit vote by claiming that it had been a "victory for real people" (thus making the 48 percent of the British electorate who had opposed taking the UK out of the European Union somehow less than real—or, put more directly, questioning their status as proper members of the political community). Or consider a remark by Donald Trump that went virtually unnoticed, given the frequency with which the New York billionaire has made outrageous and deeply offensive statements. At a campaign rally in May, Trump announced that "the only important thing is the unification of the people—because the other people don't mean anything."[35]

Since Greek and Roman times, "the people" has been used in at least three senses: first, the people as the whole (which is to say, all members of the polity, or what used to be called "the body politic"); second, the "common people" (the part of the res publica made up of commoners, or in modern terms: the excluded, the downtrodden, and the forgotten); and, third, the nation as a whole, understood in a distinctly cultural sense.[36]

It is plainly inadequate to say that all appeals to "the people" qualify as populism. An idealization of the people (think of Bakunin saying "the people is the only source of moral truth . . . and I have in mind the scoundrel, the dregs, uncontaminated by bourgeois civilization") would not necessarily be populism, though the Russian *narodniki* in the late nineteenth century understood populism in precisely this way. Less obviously, advocacy for "the common people" or the excluded—even if it involves an explicit criticism of elites—is also insufficient evidence of populism. For a political actor or movement to be populist, it must claim that a *part* of the people *is* the people— and that only the populist authentically identifies and represents this real or true people. Put in terms derived from ancient Rome, fighting for the interests of the *plebs*, "the common people," is *not* populism, but saying that only the *plebs* (as opposed to the patrician class, never mind the slaves) is the *populus Romanus*—and that only a particular kind of *populares* properly represents the authentic people—*is* populism. In the same vein, in Machiavelli's Florence, fighting for the *popolo* against the *grandi* would not automatically be populism, but saying that the *grandi* do not belong in Florence, no matter what they say or do, *would* be populism.

Populists themselves often conceive of political morality in terms of work and corruption. This has led some observers to associate populism with a distinct ideology of "producerism."[37] Populists pit the pure, innocent, always hardworking people against a corrupt elite who do not really work (other than to further their self-interest) and, in right-wing populism, also against the very bottom of society (those who also do not really work and live like parasites off the work of others). In American history, think of the way followers of Andrew Jackson opposed both "aristocrats" at the top and Native Americans and slaves below them.[38] Right-wing populists also typically claim to discern a symbiotic relationship between an elite that does not truly belong and marginal groups that are also distinct from the people. In the twentieth-century United States, these groups were usually liberal elites on the one hand and racial minorities on the other. The controversy over Barack Obama's birth certificate made this logic almost ridiculously obvious and literal: at one and the same time, the president managed to embody in the eyes of right-wingers both the "bicoastal elite" and the African American Other, neither of which really belongs to the United States proper. This helps explain the extraordinary obsession of the "birthers" with proving that Obama was not just symbolically an *illegitimate* office holder but plainly an *illegal* one—an "un-American" figure who had usurped the nation's highest office under false pretenses. (This obsession went far beyond the tendency of right-wingers during the 1990s to term Bill Clinton "your president"—though the basic impulse to cast the chief executive as fundamentally illegitimate was similar.)[39] One might also think of post-Communist elites and ethnic groups such as the Roma in Central and Eastern Europe, or "Communists" and illegal immigrants (according to Silvio Berlusconi) in Italy. In the former case, the liberal post-Communist elites do not properly belong, as they collude with outside powers such as the European Union and espouse beliefs alien to the true homeland, while the Roma—Europe's most discriminated minority— has no proper place in the nation to begin with. The far-right populist Jobbik party in Hungary, for instance, always analogizes "politician crime" and "gypsy crime."[40]

The moralistic conception of politics advanced by populists clearly depends on some criterion for distinguishing the moral and the immoral, the pure and the corrupt, the people who matter, in Trump's parlance, and those "who don't mean anything." But the distinction does not have to be work and its opposite. If "work" turns out to be indeterminate, ethnic markers can readily come to the rescue. (Of course, racist thought often equates race and laziness without having to make that equation explicit: nobody ever imagines welfare queens to be white.) Still, it's a mistake to think that populism will always turn out to be a form of nationalism or ethnic chauvinism. There are a variety of ways for a populist to distinguish moral and immoral. What will always need to be present is *some* distinction between the morally pure people and their opponents. This assumption of the noble people also then distinguishes populists from other political actors who are antipluralists. For instance, Leninists and highly intolerant religious actors do not think of the people as morally pure and unerring in its will. Not everyone who rejects pluralism is a populist.

Just What Exactly Do Populists Claim to Represent?

Contrary to conventional wisdom, populists do not have to be against the idea of representation as such; rather, they can positively endorse a particular version of it. Populists are fine with representation, as long as the right representatives represent the right people to make the right judgment and consequently do the right thing.

Apart from determining who really belongs to the people, populists therefore need to say something about the content of what the authentic people actually want. What they usually suggest is that there is a singular common good, that the people can discern and will it, and that a politician or a party (or, less plausibly, a movement) can unambiguously implement it as policy.[41] In this sense, as Cas Mudde and Cristóbal Rovira Kaltwasser have pointed out in their important work on empirical cases of populism, populist always sounds at least somewhat "Rousseauean," even if there are also important differences between populism and Rousseau's democratic thought, to which I'll turn in a moment.[42] Moreover, the emphasis on a singular common good that is clearly comprehensible to common sense and capable of being articulated as a singularly correct policy that can be collectively willed at least partly explains why populism is so often associated with the idea of an oversimplification of policy challenges.[43] Hungary's right-wing populist leader Viktor Orbán, for instance, did not participate in debates before the 2010 and 2014 elections (both of which he went on to win). He explained his refusal to debate as follows:

> No policy-specific debates are needed now, the alternatives in front of us are obvious [. . .] I am sure you have seen what happens when a tree falls over a road and many people gather around it. Here you always have two kinds of people. Those who have great ideas how to remove the tree, and share with others their wonderful theories, and give advice. Others simply realize that the best is to start pulling the tree from the road. . . . [W]e need to understand that for rebuilding the economy it is not theories that are needed but rather thirty robust lads who start working to implement what we all know needs to be done.[44]

Here Orbán equates the correct policy with what common sense can easily discern. What needs to be done is obvious; no debate about values or weighing of empirical evidence is required.

Except that it is required. We have already seen how, for populists, there cannot be such a thing as legitimate competition when populists run for office—hence slogans such as *"Abbasso tutti!"* ("Down with them all!"),

"*¡Que se vayan todos!*" ("Everyone out!"), *Qu'ils s'en aillent tous!* ("Let them all go!"), or Beppe Grillo's "V-Days" ("V" stood for *vaffanculo* [fuck off]). When they are in power, there is likewise no such thing as a legitimate opposition. But then, if they are the only legitimate representatives of the people, how can it be that populists aren't in power already? And how could anyone be against them once they have attained power? Here a crucial aspect of populists' understanding of political representation comes into play: while it can sound as if they espouse a notion of a democratic representation of the popular *will*, they actually rely on a *symbolic* representation of the "real people" (as in the notion of "real Americans," a beloved term of George Wallace). For them, "the people themselves" is a fictional entity outside existing democratic procedures, a homogeneous and morally unified body whose alleged will can be played off against actual election results in democracies. It is not an accident that Richard Nixon's famous (or infamous) notion of a "silent majority" has had such an illustrious career among populists: if the majority were not silent, it would already have a government that truly represented it.[45] If the populist politician fails at the polls, it is not because he or she does not represent the people, but because the majority has not yet dared to speak. As long they are in opposition, populists will always invoke an uninstitutionalized people "out there"—in existential opposition to officeholders who have been authorized by an actual election, or even just opinion polls, which fail to reflect what populists see as the true popular will.

Such a notion of "the people" beyond all political forms and formation was influentially theorized by the right-wing legal theorist Carl Schmitt during the interwar period. His work, together with that of Fascist philosopher Giovanni Gentile, served as a conceptual bridge from democracy to nondemocracy when they claimed that fascism could more faithfully realize and instantiate democratic ideals than democracy itself.[46] Conversely, an opponent of Schmitt such as the Austrian jurist (and democratic theorist) Hans Kelsen insisted that the will of parliament was not the popular will; and that something like an unambiguous popular will was in fact impossible to discern. All we could verify were election outcomes, and everything else, according to Kelsen (in particular an organic unity of "the people" from which some interest above parties could be inferred), amounted to a "metapolitical illusion."[47]

The term *illusion* is justified here. For the whole people can never be grasped and represented—not least because it never remains the same, not even for a minute: citizens die, new citizens are born. Yet it is always tempting to claim that one can actually know the people as such.[48] Robespierre made it easy for himself when he said that he simply was the people (in a sense that follows the logic of the kings whom the French Revolution had deposed). It is telling that the French revolutionaries never found a satisfactory way symbolically to represent the principle of popular sovereignty: the whole people could not appear as such, and particular symbols, such as the Phrygian cap, a crowned youth, or Hercules, clearly failed to convince. Jacques-Louis David wanted to erect a giant statue of "the people" on the Pont Neuf; the foundations were to be made of shattered royal monuments, and the bronze of the statue was supposed to have been furnished by the melted canons of the "enemies of the people." (The plans were approved, but only a model was constructed.) The supposedly most important actor of the revolution—the sovereign people—became the "Yahweh of the French," which is to say, utterly unrepresentable. (Only the word could be shown: at revolutionary festivals, flags bearing citations from Rousseau's *Social Contract* were to be carried around.)[49]

As it happens, we are also in a position now to clarify the major difference between populist representation of the people and Rousseau's general will. The formation of the latter requires actual participation by citizens; the populist, on the other hand, can divine the proper will of the people on the basis of what it means, for instance, to be a "real American." More *Volksgeist*, if you like, than *volonté générale*—a conception of democracy in which "substance," "spirit," or, put more straightforwardly, "true identity" decides, and not the larger number. What might initially have looked like a claim by populists to represent the will turns out to be a claim to represent something like a symbolic substance.

Yet, one might object, don't populists often demand more referenda? Yes. But one needs to be clear about what the meaning of a referendum for populists really is. They do not want people to participate continuously in politics. A referendum isn't meant to start an open-ended process of deliberation among actual citizens to generate a range of well-considered popular judgments; rather, the referendum serves to ratify what the populist leader has already discerned to be the genuine popular interest as a matter of identity, not as a matter of aggregating empirically verifiable interests. Populism without participation is an entirely coherent proposition. In fact, populists are not even inherently antielitist, if one takes the latter to mean that power should always be as widely dispersed as possible. As mentioned above, populists have no problem with representation as long as they are the representatives; similarly, they are fine with elites as long as they are the elites leading the people. Hence it is naïve to think that one has scored a decisive point against a figure like Trump if one points out that he is in fact part of the existing elite (albeit not the political elite in a narrow sense); the same is true of businessmen-turned-politicians in Europe, such as the Swiss populist Christoph Blocher. They know that they are part of the elite, and so do their supporters; what matters is their promise that as a proper elite, they will not betray the people's trust and will in fact faithfully execute the people's unambiguously articulated political agenda.

It is thus no accident that populists in power (about whom I have to say more in the next chapter) often adopt a kind of "caretaker" attitude toward an essentially passive people. Think of Berlusconi's reign in Italy: the ideal was for a Berlusconi supporter comfortably to sit at home, watch TV (preferably the channels owned by Berlusconi), and leave matters of state to the *Cavaliere*, who would successfully govern the country like a very large business corporation (which was sometimes called *azienda Italia*). There was no need to enter the piazza and participate. Or think of the second Orbán government in Hungary, from 2010 onward, which crafted a supposedly authentic national constitution (after some sham process of "national consultation" by questionnaire) but felt no need to put that constitution to a popular vote.

We are also in a better position now to understand why populists often conclude "contracts" with "the people" (the deeply populist Swiss People's Party has done so, as did Berlusconi and Haider; in the United States, some might

remember Newt Gingrich's "Contract with America").[50]
Populists assume that "the people" can speak with one voice
and issue something like an imperative mandate that tells
politicians exactly what they have to do in government (as
opposed to a free mandate, according to which representatives have to use their own judgment). Thus there is no
real need for debate, let alone the messy back-and-forth
of deliberating in Congress or other national assemblies.
The populists have always already been the faithful spokes-
persons of the real people and worked out the terms of
the contract. Yet the fact is that the imperative mandate
has not really come from the people at all; its supposedly
detailed instructions are based on an interpretation by populist politicians. Political scientists have long argued that
a completely coherent, single "popular will" is a fantasy[51]
and that no one can credibly claim, as Juan Perón used to
do, that "the political leader is the one who does what the
people want."[52] What is less obvious is that pretending that
there is such a will also weakens democratic accountability. Populists can always turn back to the people and say,
"We implemented exactly want you wanted, you authorized
us; if anything goes wrong, it's not our fault." By contrast,
a free mandate, as opposed to an imperative one, puts the
burden on representatives to justify how they used their
political judgment, when election time—that is to say, time
for accountability—comes around. Populists like to suggest
that a free mandate is somehow undemocratic; the opposite
is true, and it is not an accident that democratic constitutions that specify an understanding of representatives' role
opt for a free, and not an imperative, mandate.

Principled, moralized antipluralism and the reliance
on a noninstitutionalized notion of "the people" also helps

explain why populists so frequently oppose the "morally correct" outcome of a vote to the actual empirical result of an election, when the latter was not in their favor. Think of Victor Orbán claiming, after losing the 2002 Hungarian elections, that "the nation cannot be in opposition"; or of Andrés Manuel López Obrador arguing, after his failed bid for the Mexican presidency in 2006, that "the victory of the right is morally impossible" (and declaring himself "the legitimate president of Mexico");[53] or of Tea Party Patriots claiming that the president who won a majority of the vote is "governing against the majority."[54] Then there is the example of Geert Wilders, who has called the Dutch *Tweede Kamer* a "fake parliament" with "fake politicians." And then, finally, there is Donald Trump reacting to every loss in the primaries with the charge that his opponents were committing fraud, as well as his preemptive claim that the entire system—including the Republican National Convention itself—is "rigged." In short, the problem is never the populist's imperfect capacity to represent the people's will; rather, it's always the institutions that somehow produce the wrong outcomes. So even if they look properly democratic, there must be something going on behind the scenes that allows corrupt elites to continue to betray the people. Conspiracy theories are thus not a curious addition to populist rhetoric; they are rooted in and emerge from the very logic of populism itself.

Populist Leadership

At first sight, many populist leaders seem to confirm the expectation that they are "just like us," that they are "men (or even women) of the people." But then some leaders clearly don't fit that description. Donald Trump surely is not "just like us" in all kinds of ways; in fact, it might seem that the real populist leader is exactly the opposite of "us"—which is to say, ordinary. He or she must be charismatic, for one thing, which means endowed with extraordinary gifts. So which is it? Was Hugo Chávez just an average person? Or was he somehow special because he was "a little of all of you," as he liked to put it?

At first sight, it might appear that the basic logic of representation through the mechanism of election also applies to populists: one chooses a populist politician because of his or her *superior* capacity to discern the common good, as judged by the people.[55] This is no different from the general understanding of elections according to which the vote helps us get "the best" into office (a notion that has led some observers to argue that elections always contain an aristocratic element; if we really believed that all citizens were equal, we would employ lotteries to fill offices, just as was the case in ancient Athens).[56] The person elected might seem more likely to discern the common good because he or she shares important features with us, but this is not necessary. In any case, nobody can be "identical" with us, strictly speaking. Even "Joe the Plumber" is in a sense special because he is more ordinary than anyone.[57]

A clue to how populist leadership actually operates might be the election slogans of the Austrian far-right populist politician Heinz-Christian Strache (successor to Jörg Haider as chairman of Austrian Freedom Party): "*ER will, was WIR wollen*" ("HE wants what WE want"), which is not quite the same as "He is like you." Or another one: "*Er sagt, was Wien denkt*" ("He says, what Vienna thinks"), not "He says (or is), what Vienna is." Or, to evoke a fictional politician from a completely different part of the world, "My study is the heart of the people," which is Willie Stark's slogan in *All the King's Men* (the greatest novel on populism ever written, based loosely on Huey Long's career in Louisiana).

The leader correctly discerns what we correctly think, and sometimes he might just think the correct thing a little bit before we do. This, I would venture, is the meaning of Donald Trump's frequent imperatives issued on Twitter to "THINK!" or "GET SMART!" All this does not depend on charisma; neither does it rely on being an outsider in politics. Of course, it's more credible to run against existing elites if one isn't obviously one of them. Yet there are certainly cases where populists are clearly identifiable as nothing but career politicians: Geert Wilders and Viktor Orbán, for instance, have spent their entire adult lives within parliaments. It does not seem to have hurt their standing as populists.

But in what ways exactly do they claim to represent and also "lead" us? If the analysis presented earlier is accurate, "symbolically correct" representation matters here, too. It's not that the leader has to be particularly charismatic personally. But he or she has to provide a sense of a direct connection with the "substance" of the people and, even better, with every single individual. This is why Chávez's campaigns featured slogans such as "*¡Chávez es Pueblo!*" ("Chávez is the people!") and "*¡Chávez somos millones, tú también eres Chávez!*" ("Chávez we are millions, you are also Chávez!"). And after his death, people came together around the new imperative "*Seamos como Chávez*" ("Let's be like Chávez").

The leader does not have to "embody" the people, as statements such as "Indira is India, and India is Indira" might suggest. But a sense of direct connection and identification needs to be there. Populists always want to cut out the middleman, so to speak, and to rely as little as possible on complex party organizations as intermediaries between citizens and politicians. The same is true of wanting to be done with journalists: the media is routinely accused by populists of "mediating," which, as the very word indicates, is what they are actually supposed to do, but which is seen by populists as somehow distorting political reality. Nadia Urbinati has coined the useful, if at first sight paradoxical, concept of "direct representation" for this phenomenon.[58] A perfect example is Beppe Grillo and his Five Star Movement in Italy, which literally grew out of Grillo's blog. The ordinary Italian can check out what is really going on through direct access to Grillo's website, provide some input online, and then also come to identify with Grillo as the only authentic representative of the Italian people. As Grillo himself explained, "Folks, it works like this: You let me know, and I play the amplifier."[59] When the *grillini*—as Grillo's followers are called—finally entered parliament, Gianroberto Casaleggio, Grillo's strategist and Internet impresario, explained that "Italian public opinion" itself had at last arrived in parliament.[60]

Arguably, Donald Trump's Twitter account has had a similar lure in the 2016 presidential campaign: "real Americans" can be done with the media and have direct access (or, rather, the illusion of direct contact with) a man who is not just a celebrity; the self-declared "Hemingway of 140 characters" uniquely tells it like it is. Everything that liberals from Montesquieu and Tocqueville onward once lauded as moderating influences—what they called intermediate institutions—disappears here in favor of Urbinati's "direct representation." In the same way, everything that might contradict what we are already thinking is silenced in the echo chamber of the Internet. The web (and a leader like Trump) always have an answer—and, amazingly, it always happens to be the one we were expecting.

Principled antipluralism and the commitment to "direct representation" explain another feature of populist politics that is often commented on in isolation. I refer to the fact that populist parties are almost always internally monolithic, with the rank-and-file clearly subordinated to a single leader (or, less often, a group of leaders). Now, "internal democracy" of political parties—which some constitutions actually take to be a litmus test for democracy and hence the legitimacy (and, ultimately, legality) of parties—can be a bit of a pious hope. Many parties still are what Max Weber said they were: machines for selecting and electing leaders or, at best, arenas for personality-driven micropolitics as opposed to a forum for reasoned debate. While this is a general tendency of parties, populist parties are particularly prone to internal authoritarianism. If there is only one common good and only one way to represent it faithfully (as opposed to a self-consciously partisan but also self-consciously fallible interpretation of what the common good might be), then disagreement within the party that claims to be the sole legitimate representative of the common good obviously cannot be permissible.[61] And if there is only one "symbolically correct" representation of the real people—the understanding on which populists always fall back, as we have seen—then there's also not much point in debating that.

Geert Wilders's *Partij voor de Vrijheid* (PVV) is an extreme example. This is not just metaphorically a one-man-party; Wilders controls everything and everyone. Initially, Wilders and his chief intellectual Martin Bosma did not even want to establish a political party but a foundation. This proved legally impossible, but the PVV today operates as a party with exactly two members: Wilders himself and a foundation, *Stichting Groep Wilders*, with (one might have guessed it) once again Wilders as the only member.[62] The members of the PVV in parliament are merely delegates (and are extensively coached by Wilders every Saturday on how to present themselves and how to do their legislative work).[63] Something similar is true of Grillo. He is not just the "amplifier," as he pretends. He exercises central control over "his" parliamentary deputies and expels from the movement those who dare to disagree with him.[64]

Now, in practice, populists have compromised here and there, entered coalitions, and moderated their absolute claim to a unique representation of the people. But it would be wrong to conclude from this that they are, after all, just like all the other parties. There is a reason they want to be a "front" (as in Front National), a "movement," or indeed a foundation.[65] A party is just a part (of the people), whereas populists put forward the claim to stand for the whole, without remainder.

In practice, it is also clear that the content of the "correct symbolic representation" of the people can change over time even within the same party. Think of the Front National (FN). Under founder Jean-Marie Le Pen, the party was initially a rallying point for right-wing extremists, monarchists, and especially those who could not accept France's loss of Algeria in the 1960s. More recently, Le Pen's daughter Marine has dropped the historical revisionism of her father (who infamously called the gas chambers a "historical detail"), and tried to present her party as the last defender of French republican values against the twin threats of Islam and Eurozone economic dictatorship by Germany. Every second Sunday in May, the FN holds a rally at the statue of Jeanne d'Arc in the first district of Paris, symbolically rededicating itself to French independence and what it construes as authentic French popular sovereignty. Times have changed, and so have the ways in which "the real people" can be evoked through specifying the main enemies of *la République*.

Such transformations can be effected more easily if the central symbolic statement of the populists is virtually empty. What does "Make America Great Again" actually mean, other than that the people have been betrayed by elites and that anybody who opposes Trump must also somehow be against "American Greatness"? What did George Wallace's "Stand Up for America" (the national version of his successful slogan "Stand Up for Alabama") signify, other than that the United States was being victimized and that anyone critical of Wallace automatically failed to defend America?

One More Time: Isn't Everyone a Populist, Then?

As we have seen, populism is a distinctly moral way to imagine the political world and necessarily involves a claim to exclusive moral representation. Of course, it's not just populists who talk about morality; all political discourse is shot through with moral claims, just as virtually all political actors make what Michael Saward has called "the representative claim."[66] At the same time, few political actors go around saying, "We are just a faction; we just represent special interests." Even fewer would admit that their opponents might be just as right as they are; the logic of political competition and differentiation makes that impossible. What distinguishes democratic politicians from populists is that the former make representative claims in the form of something like hypotheses that can be empirically disproven on the basis of the actual results of regular procedures and institutions like elections.[67] Or, as Paulina Ochoa Espejo has argued, democrats make claims about the people that are self-limiting and are conceived of as fallible.[68] In some sense, they'd have to subscribe to Beckett's famous words in *Worstward Ho*: "Ever tried. Ever failed. No matter. Try again. Fail again. Fail better."

Populists, by contrast, will persist with their representative claim no matter what; because their claim is of a moral and symbolic—not an empirical—nature, it cannot be disproven. When in opposition, populists are bound to cast doubt on the institutions that produce the "morally wrong" outcomes. Hence they can accurately be described as "enemies of institutions"—although not of institutions in general. They are merely the enemies of mechanisms of representation that fail to vindicate their claim to excusive moral representation.

Nonpopulist politicians do not propose in rousing speeches to speak merely for a faction (though some do; at least in Europe, party names often indicate that the parties in question only really mean to represent a particular clientele, such as smallholders or Christians). Nor do run-of-the-mill democratic politicians necessarily subscribe to a high-minded ethics according to which, beyond all our partisan differences, we are engaged in a common project of perfecting the political community's foundational political values.[69] But most *would* concede that representation is temporary and fallible, that contrary opinions are legitimate, that society cannot be represented without remainder, and that it is impossible for one party or politicians permanently to represent an authentic people apart from democratic procedures and forms. Which means that they implicitly accept a basic claim that was clearly articulated by Habermas: "the people" appear only in the plural.[70]

To summarize, populism is not a matter of a specific psychological cast, a particular class, or simplistic policies. Neither is it just a question of style. Yes, George Wallace made a point of wearing cheap suits and telling Americans that he "put ketchup on everything." Yes, some populists test the limits of how rude one can be in a debate (or about the host of a debate). But it doesn't follow, as some social scientists hold, that we can simply and safely identify populists by their "bad manners."[71] Populism is not just any mobilization strategy that appeals to "the people";[72] it employs a very specific kind of language. Populists do not just criticize elites; they also claim that they and only they represent the true people. Whether someone speaks that language or not isn't a matter of subjective impressions. Scholars such as Keith Hawkins have systematically identified elements of populist language and even quantified its occurrence in different countries.[73] One can therefore also meaningfully speak of degrees of populism. The main point is that this populist rhetoric can be pinned down. The next question is what happens when populists put their ideas into practice.

What Populists Do, or Populism in Power

One might be tempted to conclude by now that populists live in a kind of political fantasy world: they imagine an opposition between corrupt elites and a morally pure, homogeneous people that can do no wrong; they play a symbolic representation of that people off against sordid political realities where populists do not yet rule. Aren't such fantasies bound to fail?

Conventional wisdom has it that populist parties are primarily protest parties and that protest cannot govern, since one cannot protest against oneself (and, once political actors have become an elite in power, it will simply prove impossible for them to perpetuate an antielitist stance).[1] Finally, there's the notion that populists, when they reach office, will somehow lose their nimbus; charisma will be used up and "disenchanted" in everyday parliamentary routines. Returning to an earlier (in my view, flawed) definition of populism, one might think that the simplistic prescriptions of populists will also quickly be exposed as unworkable. Antipolitics cannot generate real policies.

The notion that populists in power are bound to fail one way or another is comforting. It's also an illusion. For one thing, while populist parties do indeed protest against elites, this does not mean that populism in government will become contradictory. First of all, all failures of populists in government can still be blamed on elites acting behind the scenes, whether at home or abroad (here we see again the not-so-accidental connection between populism and conspiracy theories). Many populist victors continue to behave like victims; majorities act like mistreated minorities. Chávez would always point to the dark machinations of the opposition—the officially deposed "oligarchy"—trying to sabotage his "twenty-first century socialism." (When that did not seem plausible, he could always hold the United States responsible for any failures of the Bolivarian Revolution.) Recep Tayyip Erdoğan has likewise presented himself as a plucky underdog; he would always be the street fighter from Istanbul's tough neighborhood Kasımpaşa, bravely confronting the old Kemalist establishment of the Turkish republic—even long after he had begun to concentrate all political, economic, and cultural power in his own hands.

Populists in office continue to polarize and prepare the people for nothing less than what is conjured up as a kind of apocalyptic confrontation. They seek to moralize political conflict as much as possible (for Chávez, George W. Bush was nothing less than the devil himself, as he declared on the world stage at a session of the United Nations). There is never a dearth of enemies—and these are always nothing less than enemies of the people as a whole. Chávez declared in the midst of a general strike initiated by the opposition in 2002, "This is not about pro-Chávez and anti-Chávez ... but ... the patriots against the enemies of the homeland."[2] A "crisis" is not an objective state of affairs but a matter of interpretation. Populist will often eagerly frame a situation as a crisis, calling it an existential threat, because such a crisis then serves to legitimate populist governance. Put differently, a "crisis" can be a performance, and politics can be presented as a continuous state of siege.[3] Figures like Chávez and Ecuador's Rafael Correa understand governing as a permanent campaign—which, to be sure, is an attitude also found among nonpopulist politicians. Yet Correa goes several steps further in conceiving of his role as president as that of a permanent "motivator."[4]

Populists combine this constant creation of pressure with an aesthetic production of "proximity to the people." Viktor Orbán has himself interviewed on Hungarian radio every Friday; Chávez hosted the famous show *Aló Presidente*, in which ordinary citizens could phone in and tell the country's leader about their worries and concerns. The president would then sometimes give government members in attendance seemingly spontaneous instructions. (Chávez once told his defense minister live on air to dispatch ten tank battalions to the Columbian border.) Every now and then, welfare measures would be announced in front of the rolling cameras; the show sometimes lasted for up to six hours. Today, Correa and Bolivian president Evo Morales take part in their own similar TV programs.[5]

One can dismiss such practices as a curious kind of political folklore or, in fact, as similar to the public relations that have become mandatory for all politicians in what has been described as the "media democracy" or "audience democracy" of our time (in which citizens engage in political activity primarily by watching the powerful).[6] It is also true, however, that populists employ very particular techniques of governing—and that these techniques can be justified morally with reference to the core logic of populism. Populists in power invariably fall back on the argument that they are the only morally legitimate representatives of the people and that, furthermore, only some of the people are actually the real, authentic people who are deserving of support and, ultimately, good government. This logic can manifest itself in three distinct ways: a kind of colonization of the state, mass clientelism as well as what political scientists sometimes call "discriminatory legalism," and, finally, the systematic repression of civil society. It is not just populists who engage in such practices; what is distinctive about populists is that they can do so quite openly. They claim to have a moral justification for their conduct, and on the international stage, at least, they have a good chance of maintaining a reputation as democrats. Exposing these practices for what they are is not nearly as damaging for populists as one might think, since they will merely assert that they are implementing a proper conception of democracy. Let me spell out these seemingly counterintuitive claims in some more detail.

Three Populist Techniques for Governing and Their Moral Justifications

First, populists tend to colonize or "occupy" the state. Think of Hungary and Poland as recent examples. One of the first fundamental changes Viktor Orbán and his Fidesz Party sought was a transformation of the civil service law, so as to enable the party to place loyalists in what should have been nonpartisan bureaucratic positions. Both Fidesz and Jarosław Kaczyński's Law and Justice Party (PiS) also immediately moved against the independence of courts. Procedures of existing courts were amended and new judges were appointed. Where a reshaping of the entire system proved difficult, as has been the case in Poland so far, paralysis of the judiciary proved an acceptable second best for the governing party. Media authorities were also immediately captured; the clear signal went out that journalists should not report in ways that violate the interests of the nation (which were of course equated with the interests of the governing party). For Kaczyński, who has long believed that a shadowy "network" is bent on undermining his party, it was also crucial to bring the secret services under control. Whoever criticized any of these measures was vilified as doing the bidding of the old elites (which the populists as proper representatives of the people had finally managed to replace) or as being outright traitors (Kaczyński spoke of "Poles of the worst sort" who supposedly have "treason in their genes"). The end result is that political parties create a state to their own political liking and in their own political image.

Such a strategy to consolidate or even perpetuate power is not the exclusive preserve of populists, of course. What is special about populists is that they can undertake such colonization openly and with the support of their core claim to moral representation of the people. Why, populists can ask indignantly, should the people not take possession of their state through their only rightful representatives? Why should those who obstruct the genuine popular will in the name of civil service neutrality not be purged? The state rightfully belongs to the people;

it should not confront them as something like an alien apparatus—rather, the people should properly take possession of it.

Second, populists tend to engage in mass clientelism: the exchange of material and immaterial favors by elites for mass political support. Again, such conduct is not exclusive to populists: many parties reward their clientele for turning up at the voting booths, though few would go so far as Austrian arch-populist Jörg Haider, who would literally hand out hundred-euro bills to "his people" on the streets in Carinthia. Some observers have held that, from a realist perspective, mass clientelism and early forms of democracy are more or less the same thing—for clientelism establishes some meaningful political reciprocity and allows for some modicum of accountability.[7] What makes populists distinctive, once more, is that they can engage in such practices openly and with public moral justifications, since for them only some people are really *the* people and hence deserving of the support by what is rightfully their state.

Similarly, only some of the people should get to enjoy the full protection of the laws; those who do not belong to the people or, for that matter, who might be suspected of actively working against the people, should be treated harshly. (This is "discriminatory legalism," the view that "for my friends, everything; for my enemies, the law.")[8]

Some populists got lucky in that they had resources freely available to engage in mass clientelism and even effectively build up entire classes to support their regimes. Chávez benefited crucially from the oil boom.[9] For regimes in Central and Eastern Europe especially, funds from the European Union have been equivalent to oil for some Arab authoritarian states: governments can strategically employ the subsidies to buy support or at least keep citizens quiet. What's more, they can form social strata that conform to their image of the ideal people and that are loyal to the regime. Chávez created the *Boliburguesía*, which did very well indeed as a result of the "Bolivarian Revolution." Erdoğan continues to enjoy the unshakeable support of an Anatolian middle class that emerged with the economic boom under his Justice and Development (AK) Party. (This middle class also embodies the image of an ideal, devoutly Muslim Turk, as opposed to Westernized, secular elites on the one hand and minorities such as the Kurds on the other.) Hungary's Fidesz has built up a new group that combines economic success, family values (having children brings many benefits), and religious devotion into a whole that conforms to Orbán's vision of a "Christian-national" culture.[10]

Once again, state colonization, mass clientelism, and discriminatory legalism are phenomena that can be found in many historical situations. Yet in populist regimes, they are practiced openly and, one might suspect, with a clean moral conscience. Hence also the curious phenomenon that revelations about what can only be called corruption simply do not seem to damage the reputation of populist leaders as much as one would expect. Haider's Freedom Party and the Italian Lega Nord turned out to be far more corrupt than traditional elites they had long criticized; yet both still thrive today (so much so that the Lega Nord has now replaced Berlusconi's party as the main right-wing opposition in Italy). Erdoğan, the self-declared "Man of the Nation" (*Milletin Adamı*) remains untouched by corruption scandals. Clearly, the perception among supporters of populists is that corruption and cronyism are not genuine problems as long as they look like measures pursued for the sake of a moral, hardworking "us" and not for the immoral or even foreign "them." Hence it is a pious hope for liberals to think that all they have to do is expose corruption to discredit populists. They also have to show that for the vast majority, populist corruption yields no benefits, and that a lack of democratic accountability, a dysfunctional bureaucracy, and a decline in the rule of law will in the long run hurt the people—all of them.

There is one more element of populist statecraft that is important to understand. Populists in power tend to be harsh (to say the least) with nongovernmental organizations (NGOs) that criticize them. Again, harassing or even suppressing civil society is not a practice exclusive to populists. But for them, opposition from within civil society creates a particular moral and symbolic problem: it potentially undermines their claim to exclusive moral representation of the people. Hence it becomes crucial to argue (and supposedly "prove") that civil society isn't civil society at all, and that what can seem like popular opposition has nothing to do with the proper people. This explains why rulers like Vladimir Putin in Russia, Viktor Orbán in Hungary, and PiS in Poland have gone out of their way to try to discredit NGOs as being controlled by outside powers (and declare them "foreign agents"). In a sense, they try to make the unified (and passive) people in whose name they speak a reality on the ground by silencing or discrediting those who dissent from the populist leader's construal of the people (and, sometimes, by giving them every incentive to leave the country and thereby to separate themselves from the people).[11] Put differently, a PiS government or a Fidesz government will not only create a PiS state or a Fidesz state; it will also seek to bring into existence a PiS people and a Fidesz people (often by establishing a kind of proxy, government-friendly civil society). Populists create the homogeneous people in whose name they had been speaking all along.

And that leads to a final great irony. Populism in power brings about, reinforces, or offers another variety of the very exclusion and the usurpation of the state that it most opposes in the reigning establishment it seeks to replace.[12] What the "old establishment" or "corrupt, immoral elites" supposedly have always done, the populists will also end up doing—only, one would have thought, without guilt and with a supposedly democratic justification.

Does Populism in Power Equal "Illiberal Democracy"?

Now, if one follows my account up until this point, one may well wonder, Why do populists not go all the way when it comes to regime change? If they truly believe what they say—that they are the only legitimate representatives of the people—why do they not dispense with elections altogether? If all other contenders for power are illegitimate, why not exclude them from the political game completely?

The answer to this puzzle is necessarily somewhat speculative. We know that many of the populists who have come to power continuously test their limits: a change in the election laws here, some pressure on unfriendly media there, an extra tax audit for a pesky

NGO—but nothing that looks like a rupture with democracy altogether. Of course, we do not know their thinking and their exact calculations. But it seems plausible that, in their minds at least, the costs of open authoritarianism are simply too high. *Officially* abolishing or at least suspending democracy comes with enormous loss of international reputation (and possibly loss of international material support, though, as the recent examples of Egypt and Thailand demonstrate, even what looks like the advent of old-fashioned military-bureaucratic dictatorship need not lead to a complete break of ties to the international community).

In the face of such pulling-back from outright authoritarianism, many observers have been tempted to call regimes like Turkey's and Hungary's "illiberal democracies." Yet this designation is deeply misleading and in fact undermines attempts to rein in populist actors. "Illiberal democracy" leaves governments like Kaczyński's, Orbán's, or Maduro's in the position of claiming that their countries are still democracies, just not liberal ones. This is not just some petty semantic point; outside observers should be absolutely clear that it is democracy itself that populism damages. Given the prevalence of the diagnosis of "illiberal democracy" among political scientists and policy analysts, let me explain in some detail why it is wrongheaded.

The term *illiberal democracy* became popular in Western policy circles in the mid-1990s as a way of describing regimes that held elections but did not observe the rule of law and violated checks and balances in particular. In a highly influential article, the American journalist Fareed Zakaria claimed that governments with popular backing were regularly breaching the principles of what he called "constitutional liberalism." The latter included political rights, civil liberties, and property rights. The diagnosis of "illiberal democracy" was one symptom of a general philosophical and political hangover after 1989. In the heady days when Communism fell and the world seemed drunk on democracy, it appeared that majority rule and the rule of law would always go neatly together. But soon elections produced majorities that then used all the available power to oppress minorities and violate fundamental rights. The clear implication was that liberalism had to be strengthened to contain the dangers of democracy in countries where the political contenders exhibit a "winner-take-all" mentality.

This conceptual split between liberalism and democracy was not exactly a new one. Both left-wing and right-wing critics of "bourgeois democracy" have long operated with it. Very broadly speaking, Marxists charged that under capitalism, liberalism offered mere "formal freedoms" and a kind of fake political emancipation while effectively protecting what was often referred to as the "private autonomy" of citizens (which is to say, it secured their status as participants in the market and gave the state the role of enforcer of contracts). On the right, Carl Schmitt, in the course of the 1920s, claimed that liberalism was an outdated ideology: in the nineteenth century, it had justified elites rationally debating policies in parliament, but in the age of mass democracy, parliaments were a mere façade for sordid deals among special interests. By contrast, the genuine popular will could be represented by a leader such as Mussolini. Acclamation by a homogeneous people became the hallmark of proper democracy, which Schmitt defined as "the identity of governed and governing"; unelected institutions such as constitutional courts might be understood as guardians of liberalism, but they were essentially undemocratic.

Schmitt also performed a fateful conceptual split between the "substance" of the people on the one hand and the empirical outcome of elections or opinion surveys on the other—the very split populists regularly use, as I argued in the previous chapter. It is worth quoting Schmitt here in full because his thought explains many recent shifts to authoritarianism under the guise of democratic-sounding language:

> The unanimous opinion of one hundred million private persons is neither the will of the people nor public opinion. The will of the people can be expressed just as well and perhaps better through acclamation, through something taken for granted, an obvious and unchallenged presence, than through the statistical apparatus that has been constructed with such meticulousness in the last fifty years. The stronger the power of democratic feeling, the more certain is the awareness that democracy is something other than a registration system for secret ballots. Compared to a democracy that is direct, not only in the technical sense but also in a vital sense, parliament appears an artificial machinery, produced by liberal reasoning, while dictatorial and Caesaristic methods not only can produce the acclamation of the people but can also be a direct expression of democratic substance and power.[13]

More recently, critics of the supposed hegemony of liberalism in the post-1989 world—most prominently the left-wing theorist Chantal Mouffe—have argued that "rationalist" liberal thought has come to deny the legitimacy of conflict and disagreement, which is inherent in democracy. At the same time, Social Democratic parties have abandoned the task of offering a real alternative to neoliberalism; their convergence on a "Third Way" reinforced the sense among voters that they were being offered "elections without choice" (or, as Mouffe once put it in an interview, a mere choice between Coke and Pepsi). According to Mouffe, this convergence of political parties, as well as the compulsion to reach consensus—which allegedly can be found in the democratic theories of John Rawls and Jürgen Habermas—has provoked strong antiliberal countermovements, most prominently right-wing populism.

Beyond these debates in political theory, "liberalism"—at least in Europe, though not in the United States—has come to stand for unfettered capitalism; very much like in the United States, it has also turned into shorthand for maximizing the freedom of personal lifestyles. After the financial crisis, a new wave of self-declared antiliberals used the ambiguities surrounding the "L-word" to make the case for a different form of democracy. Erdoğan, emphasizing traditional Islamic morality, started to present himself as a "conservative democrat." Orbán, in a controversial speech in 2014, unveiled his project of creating an "illiberal state." More recently, during the refugee crisis, the Hungarian leader has announced that the era of what he simply called "liberal blah blah" in Europe was over and that the continent would come around to his "Christian and national" vision of politics.[14] "Illiberalism" here appears to mean both opposing unfettered capitalism, where the strong are always bound to win, and countering the extension of rights to minorities such as homosexuals. It is about restrictions in both markets and morals.

Now, "illiberal democracy" is not necessarily a contradiction in terms. Throughout the nineteenth and twentieth centuries, many European Christian Democrats would have called themselves "illiberal"; in fact, they might have been offended if one questioned their staunch antiliberalism. But this did not mean that they failed to understand how important the rights of political minorities are in a functioning democracy (after all, minorities can become the majority in the next election); on the contrary, they knew firsthand what it might mean for minorities not to be protected from the powerful, as Catholics had become the victims of aggressive cultural campaigns waged by secular states (think of Bismarck's *Kulturkampf* in late-nineteenth-century Germany). They also did not think that unelected institutions like courts were somehow undemocratic; once again, they themselves had sympathy for the idea of checks and balances because they had experienced what unbridled popular sovereignty can mean for religious minorities. The reason, then, was simply that they associated "liberalism" with individualism, materialism and, very often, atheism. (Think, for instance, of Jacques Maritain, the leading French Catholic philosopher and one of the authors of the United Nations Declaration of Human Rights. He argued that democracy could be endorsed on specifically Catholic grounds, while liberalism had to be rejected.) For thinkers like this, being "antiliberal" did not mean lack of respect for basic political rights, but it did signal a critique of capitalism—even if Christian Democrats did not question the legitimacy of private property as such—as well as an emphasis on a traditional, patriarchal understanding of the family.

There can be nonliberal philosophical underpinnings of democracy, as in the case of Maritain. And there can be traditional societies in which rights to abortion and marriage are highly restricted. I believe that for good reasons one should oppose the latter, but it would be peculiar to argue that such rights restrictions demonstrate a serious lack of democracy. If anything, one might want to talk about relatively intolerant—in that sense, illiberal—societies, but that is different from illiberal democracy. We have to distinguish illiberal societies from places where freedom of speech and assembly, media pluralism, and the protection of minorities are under attack. These political rights are not just about liberalism (or the rule of law); they are constitutive of democracy as such. For instance, even if ballots are not stuffed by the ruling party on the day of the election, a vote can be undemocratic if the opposition can never make its case properly and journalists are prevented from reporting a government's failures. Even for the most minimal definitions of democracy—as a mechanism to ensure peaceful turnovers in power after a process of popular will-formation—it is crucial that citizens be well informed about politics; otherwise, governments can hardly be held accountable. It is not an accident that many new democracies after 1989 established constitutional courts to protect basic political rights and preserve pluralism in politics and society. Such courts, the justification went, ultimately helped the flourishing of democracy itself (and not just liberalism).

If critics keep invoking "illiberal democracy," leaders like Orbán will simply say, "Thank you very much."

The supposed criticism confirms the Hungarian prime minister as exactly what he wants to be: an opponent of liberalism. At the same time, he, Kaczyński, and all other populist leaders get to keep "democracy," which, for all the disappointments over the last quarter-century, remains the most important ticket to recognition on the global stage. Even better from the point of view of such leaders, the expression "illiberal democracy" confirms a normative division of labor, where the nation-state does democracy, and an entity like the European Union (EU) gets to be in charge of liberalism. The EU then can then be made to look even more like an agent of rampant capitalism and libertarian morality (as in "Gayropa," the charge promoted by many homophobic enemies of the EU in Russia). Populist governments, meanwhile, can present themselves as resisting a hegemonic liberalism in the name of diversity and even minority rights, as if to say, "We Hungarians, Poles, and so on, are a minority in the EU who believe in traditional morals and do not submit to the one-size-must-fit-all liberal universalism promoted by Western liberal elites." Just think of Polish foreign minister Witold Waszczykowski, in an interview with a German tabloid in January 2016, railing against the vision of "a new mixing of cultures and races, a world of bicyclists and vegetarians, who . . . fight every form of religion." Here a vulnerable or perhaps even persecuted minority appears to be defending itself—when in fact, the minister is speaking for a government that has a majority in parliament.

All of this means we should stop the thoughtless invocation of "illiberal democracy." Populists damage democracy as such, and the fact that they have won elections does not give their projects automatic democratic legitimacy (especially because they usually haven't mentioned far-reaching constitutional changes in the campaigns that brought them to power). While they may have won an initial election fair and square, they quickly start tampering with the institutional machinery of democracy in the name of the so-called real people (as opposed to their political opponents, who are automatically deemed traitors to the nation). This people is assumed to be a homogeneous whole that can be authentically represented only by populists. In Carl Schmitt's terms, symbolic substance wins over mere numbers (of votes) that can be ascertained by what Schmitt called the statistical apparatus; the supposed authentic national will trumps procedures and delegitimizes all opposition—or, as a PiS member of parliament put it, "Above the law stands the good of the nation."

In short, populism distorts the democratic process. And if the governing party has a sufficient majority, it can enact a new constitution justified as an effort to appropriate the state for the "real Hungarians" or "real Poles," as opposed to post-Communist or liberal elites that supposedly rob the people of their own country. Of course, it helps that these former elites often simultaneously stand for economic liberalism, a pluralistic and tolerant "open society," and the protection of fundamental rights (including the rights constitutive of democracy). Orbán can then criticize the open society by saying that "there is no homeland any more, only an investment site." In Poland, German economic interests, the supposedly evil "gender ideology," and the civil society organizations defending the constitution can all be conflated and attacked at the same time. In short, anticapitalism, cultural nationalism, and authoritarian politics become inextricably linked.

Having said that, just as an overly inclusive notion of democracy is unhelpful in understanding the political reality we face, defining the concept of authoritarianism too broadly can be problematic and produce unintended political consequences. In the first case, the Hungarian and Polish governments can rejoice that they are still democracies; in the second, highly repressive regimes will be pleased if they find themselves in the same category as Hungary and Poland. In the latter, it remains perfectly possible to demonstrate on the streets, publish critical blog posts, or found new political parties. The game is being rigged, but it is not impossible—yet—to win an election on the basis of criticizing the populists in power. Perhaps, then, a designation like "defective democracy" would be more appropriate.[15] Democracy has been damaged and is in need of serious repair, but it would be misleading and premature to speak of dictatorship.

It is also important for the EU to be clear about what it is doing when it engages supposed "illiberal democracies" like Hungary and Poland. Most of its activities have been framed as "protecting the rule of law." The European Commission's new approach, unveiled in 2014, is known as the "rule of law mechanism." It seeks initially to establish a dialogue about the rule of law with a member state that is suspected of breaching the values codified in Article 2 of the Treaty on European Union (the rule of law is among these values). The hope is that through dialogue—and not sanctions—a member state will mend its ways. In many of its publications, the commission has insisted that the rule of law and democracy are interconnected: one cannot be had without the other. Yet the virtually exclusive emphasis on rule of law in public discourse has, arguably, reinforced the sense that Europe only cares about liberalism, while the nation-state does democracy. European officials should emphasize that their concern is as much with democracy as with protecting the rule of law.

Critics of developments in Hungary and Poland, moreover, should face up to the fact that "liberalism" has often been experienced not just as cutthroat market competition but as powerful (Western European) interests getting their way. While the reality in Hungary has been savage cuts to the welfare state, Orbán's self-presentation as a strong leader ready to nationalize companies and use the state to protect ordinary folk from multinationals has been highly effective. Before he settled on the ideology of the "illiberal state," he waxed lyrical about a "plebeian democracy." This is propaganda, but it resonates because of the way a seeming convergence of political, economic, and moral liberalism was experienced after 1989. If something called liberalism can look like it's only good for winners, liberals have to rethink their commitments. As the former Hungarian dissident G. M. Tamás put it in 2009, "We, the froth at the top of it, were celebrating the triumph of freedom and openness and plurality and fantasy and pleasure and all that. That was frivolous, and I am deeply ashamed."

Those defending democracy against populism also have to be honest about the fact that all is not well with existing democracies in Western Europe and North America. To be sure, these are not mere "façade democracies," as the German social scientist Wolfgang Streeck has put it recently. They have not been captured by single parties trying to remold the entire political system in their favor, as has been the case in Hungary. But they are increasingly suffering from the defect that weaker socioeconomic groups do not participate in the political process and do not have their interests represented effectively. Again, it would be wrong simply to equate this problem with the conscious curtailing of rights constitutive of democracy and the exclusion of oppositional forces that I have claimed are characteristic of populist regimes. There can be meaningful changes in power, unlike in the situation for which Fidesz and PiS are evidently striving. But while the contrasts among contestants for power amount to more than the differences between Coke and Pepsi, critics like Mouffe have a point that needs to be answered. As David Ost has put it starkly in an analysis of the 2015 PiS victory, "The problem . . . is not that people are not committed to democracy. Yes, plenty of people today *aren't* committed to democracy but they're not committed to it because they feel that democracy, packed in neoliberal wrapping, is not committed to them." A defense of democracy today has to grapple with this challenge no less than the task of exposing the phony justifications of "plebeian democracy" and the "illiberal state."

Populist Constitutions: A Contradiction in Terms?

Despite the great divergence of approaches to understanding populism, it is striking that many observers appear to agree on one point—namely, that whatever else it is, populism is inherently hostile to the mechanisms and, ultimately, the values commonly associated with constitutionalism: constraints on the will of the majority, checks and balances, protections for minorities, and even fundamental rights.[16] Populists are supposedly impatient with procedures; they are even said to be "against institutions as such," preferring a direct, unmediated relationship between the personal leader and the people. Related to this supposed anti-institutionalism is the charge that populists dislike representation and opt instead for direct democracy (as exemplified by referenda)—a charge we already encountered and to some degree dismissed in chapter 1. Hence also the impression—widespread among both political philosophers and social scientists—that populism, despite some serious flaws, might under some circumstances serve as a "corrective" to a liberal democracy that has become too remote from the people.

This hope is misplaced, but one can see how it arose when one considers the ways in which the debate about liberal constitutionalism and populism suffers from several unfortunate characteristics. First, the discussion often becomes conflated with the controversy about the merits of majoritarianism (and, conversely, judicial review). Second, there is no clear or even discernible distinction between *popular* constitutionalism on the one hand and *populist* constitutionalism on the other.[17] And third and most important, "populism" serves as a very imprecise placeholder for "civic participation" or "social mobilization" (and, conversely, weakening the power of judges and other elites).[18] Quite apart from the vagueness of the notions used (or perhaps because of this vagueness), there's the additional fact that debates about populism and constitutionalism—especially in the United States— quickly turn emotional, with accusations of elitism or "demophobia" flying about and theorists accused of having bad "attitudes toward the political energy of ordinary people" or of promoting "ochlocracy."[19]

As hopefully has become clear by now, populists are not generally "against institutions," and they are not destined to self-destruct once in power. They only oppose those institutions that, in their view, fail to produce the morally (as opposed to empirically) correct political outcomes. And that happens only when they are in opposition. Populists in power are fine with institutions—which is to say, *their* institutions.

Those populists who have enough power will seek to establish a new populist constitution—in both the sense of a new sociopolitical settlement and a new set of rules for the political game (what some scholars of constitutionalism have called the "operating manual" of politics). It is tempting to think that with the latter, they will seek a system that allows for the expression of an unconstrained popular will or somehow reinforce the direct, institutionally unmediated relationship between a leader and the proper *pueblo*. Populists are, after all, often deemed to be heirs of the Jacobins.

Yet here again, things are not so simple. The claim for an unconstrained popular will is plausible for populists when they are in opposition; after all, they aim to pit an authentic expression of the *populus* as uninstitutionalized, nonproceduralized *corpus mysticum* against the actual results of an existing political system. In such circumstances, it is also plausible for them to say that the *vox populi* is one—and that checks and balances, divisions of power, and so on, cannot allow the singular, homogeneous will of the singular, homogeneous people to emerge clearly.

Yet when in power, populists tend to be much less skeptical about constitutionalism as a means of creating constraints on what they interpret to be the popular will—except that the popular will (never given empirically, but always construed morally) has first to be ascertained by populists, and then appropriately constitutionalized. Or, picking up a distinction developed by Martin Loughlin, positive, or constructive, constitutionalism is followed by negative, or restraining, constitutionalism.[20] Populists will seek to perpetuate what they regard as the proper image of the morally pure people (the proper constitutional identity, if you will) and then constitutionalize policies that supposedly conform to their image of the people. Hence populist constitutionalism will not necessarily privilege popular participation, nor will populists always try somehow to "constitutionalize the charisma" of a popular leader in the way that Bruce Ackerman has suggested.[21]

Apart from these features—which are explained yet again by the underlying moral claims of populism—there is a more mundane goal that constitutions might achieve for populists: they can help to keep populists in power. Of course, one might say that even this goal still has a moral dimension related to the underlying populist imagination: as the only legitimate representatives of the people, populists *should* perpetually be in office. And if the perpetuation of power becomes the aim, then there is also the possibility that populists will treat the constitution as a mere façade, while operating quite differently behind that façade.[22] Perhaps they will even sacrifice their own constitution if it no longer serves that purpose. Here the Jacobins really are the appropriate example. As Dan Edelstein has shown, their concern was much less with a faithful expression of the general will than historians have tended to assume.[23] The Jacobins worried about corruptions of the general will and put their hope in the realization of a form of natural right altogether independent of people's actual wills (and attendant frailties). When their own constitution—and the elections it enabled—threatened to remove the Jacobins from power, they did not hesitate effectively to suspend the constitution and unleash terror against those deemed *hors la loi.*

Not all examples of populist constitutionalism are as dramatic (let alone terroristic) as this. A recent example is the constitution—officially named the "Fundamental Law"—of Hungary, which came into effect at the beginning of 2012. The constitution had been preceded by a nonbinding "national consultation" to which, according to the government, about 920,000 citizens responded.[24] The outcome of that consultation could be freely interpreted by the constitution makers to fit their general conception that the 2010 parliamentary elections had resulted in what the winning party called a "revolution at the voting booths" because it had received a two-thirds majority in parliament (but only 53 percent of the actual vote, which meant 2.7 million voters out of 8 million eligible ones). This "revolution" had supposedly yielded an imperative mandate to establish what the government termed a new "National System of Cooperation" as well as a new constitution. Victor Orbán explained, "The people . . . gave good advice, good command to the Hungarian Parliament [in adopting the basic law], which it carried out. In this sense, when the Hungarian constitution is criticized . . . it is not meant for the government but for the Hungarian people . . . It is not the government the European Union has a problem with, much as they want us to believe . . .

the truth is they attack Hungary."[25] These equations—whoever attacks the government attacks the Hungarian people—are breathtaking. They are also pedagogically quite helpful, for they demonstrate the logic of populism with rare purity.

The preamble of the new constitution, or "National Creed," ended up constitutionalizing a very particular image of the Hungarian people as a nation committed to survival in a hostile world, as good Christians, and as an ethnic group that could be clearly distinguished from minorities "living with" the proper Hungarians. In the construction of the more technical constitutional machinery, the perpetuation of populists in power was clearly the goal.[26] Age limitations and qualifications for judges were introduced so as to remove professionals not in line with the governing populist party, the competences and structure of the constitutional court (a crucial check on government power before the introduction of the Fundamental Law) were reengineered, and the terms of officeholders chosen by the governing party were made unusually long (nine years in many cases), with a view, apparently, toward constraining future governments.

The Hungarian government, then, essentially designed what a former judge on the German constitutional court, Dieter Grimm, has called an "exclusive constitution," or what one might also term a *partisan* constitution: the constitution sets a number of highly specific policy preferences in stone, when debate about such preferences would have been the stuff of day-to-day political struggle in non-populist democracies.[27] Moreover, it excluded opposition parties in a double sense: they did not take part in writing or passing the constitution, and their political goals cannot be realized in the future, since the constitution highly constrains room for policy choices. In other words, under the new regime, the constitution makers can perpetuate their power even after losing an election.

The Hungarian Fundamental Law, while supposedly inspired by the views expressed in the national consultation, was never put to a referendum. By contrast, a number of new constitutions in Latin America have been created by elected constituent assemblies and were eventually made subject to a popular vote: Venezuela, Ecuador, and Bolivia are the well-known examples.[28] Older constitutions were effectively bypassed in the process of forming a constituent assembly and then replaced by documents that were supposed to perpetuate the founding "popular will." That founding will was always decisively shaped by populists. Chávez, for instance, controlled the way "his" constituent assembly was elected and ensured that a majority of 60 percent for his party at the polls translated into more than 90 percent of the seats in the constituent assembly.

Effectively, the populist ideal became reality in the form of strengthening the executive while diminishing the power of the judiciary and/or staffing judicial offices with partisan actors. Thus the new constitutions helped decisively in the populist project of "occupying the state," as the shift to a new constitution justified the replacement of existing office holders.[29] In general, elections were made less free and fair, and the media became more easily controlled by executives. As in the case of Hungary, then, the *nuevo constitucionalismo* used constitutions to set up conditions for the perpetuation of populist power, all in the name of the idea that they and only they represented *la voluntad constituyente*—the single constitutionalizing will.

Now, none of this means that populist constitutions will always work precisely as intended. They are designed to disable pluralism, but as long as populist regimes hold elections with some chance of oppositions winning, pluralism will not entirely disappear. However, such populist constitutions are then likely to result in severe constitutional conflicts. Think of the situation in Venezuela after the opposition alliance Mesa de la Unidad Democrática (MUD) emerged victorious from the December 2015 elections, gaining nothing less than a majority to change the constitution. President Maduro initially threatened to govern without parliament (but with the military); he also did everything to contest the legitimacy of three elected opposition deputies (so as to prevent the opposition from reaching the threshold required to change the constitution). The power of the executive—already strengthened enormously by Chávez in "his" constitution— was enlarged yet again so that Maduro could appoint or depose directors of the central bank as he saw fit without any involvement of parliament.[30] But that was not enough: Maduro also sought to create a kind of counterparliament in the form of a "Parliament of Communes." (A similar project of generating legitimacy parallel to the official parliament through the formation of so-called Bolivarian circles was first tried by Chávez himself and had largely failed.)[31] MUD in turn is committed to hold a referendum in order to bring down Maduro.

The point is this: Populist constitutions are designed to limit the power of nonpopulists, even when the latter form the government. Conflict then becomes inevitable. The constitution ceases to be a framework for politics and instead is treated as a purely partisan instrument to capture the polity.

Can the People Never Say "We the People"?

It might seem that the implications of the analysis so far must be profoundly conservative: politics should be confined to an interaction of official political institutions, whatever these institutions produce by way of empirical outcomes must be legitimate, and claims *about, for,* let alone *by* the people are prohibited. But this would be a misunderstanding. In a democracy, anybody can launch a representative claim and see whether a particular constituency is responsive to it—or, for that matter, whether any constituency will identify with the symbolic rendering of a group identity of which citizens hadn't been conscious at all. In fact, one might even say that democracy is precisely designed to multiply such claims: the conduct of official representatives should be contestable, and the contestation may involve the argument that the representatives fail to represent—which may mean that they fail to act for their constituents or that they even violate the symbolic self-understanding of the political community.[32]

Street protest, online petitions, and so on—these all have genuinely democratic meaning, but they lack proper democratic form, and they cannot yield a kind of democratic trump card against representative institutions.[33] In any case, such contestation is different from attempts to speak in the name of the people as a whole—and efforts to morally delegitimize all those who in turn contest that claim.

But what about those struggling in the name of "people power" in various parts of the world? To take a recent example, the demonstrators against the Mubarak regime in Tahrir Square used expressions such as "One hand," "One society," and "One demand." (There were also more creative slogans, such as "The people want a president who does not dye his hair!")[34] Should they be lectured and told that, unfortunately, they had failed properly to understand democracy and were fated to misconstrue constitutionalism?

The analysis presented in this book does not in any way exclude claims about exclusions, so to speak. Anyone can criticize existing procedures, fault them for moral blind spots, and propose criteria and means for further inclusion. What is problematic is not the claim that present arrangements have failed but the claim that the critic and *only the critic* can speak for "the people." What is problematic is also the assumption—prevalent but neither empirically nor normatively justified—by many self-declared radical democratic theorists that *only* the *pars pro toto* claim can achieve anything truly worthwhile for the previously excluded, and that everything else will amount to mere administration or cooptation into existing political and social arrangements.[35] This perspective fails to see that a claim of "we and only we represent the people" might sometimes help political actors gain power but then make securing the long-term stability of a polity all the more difficult. Once the stakes are raised to the level of nonnegotiable identity claims, continuous conflict appears likely.

It is almost a cliché to point out that many constitutions have evolved because of struggles for inclusion and because ordinary "citizen interpreters" of the constitution have sought to redeem previously unrealized moral claims contained in a founding document.[36] The not-so-trivial point is that those fighting for inclusion have rarely claimed "We *and only we* are the people." On the contrary, they have usually claimed "We are *also* the people" (with attendant claims of "we *also* represent the people" by various leaders). Constitutions with democratic principles allow for an open-ended contestation of what those principles might mean in any given period; they allow new publics to come into being on the basis of a novel claim to representation. Citizens who never thought of themselves as having much in common can respond to an unsuspected appeal to being represented and all of a sudden see themselves as a collective actor—as individuals capable of acting in concert (to invoke an expression made famous by Hannah Arendt). Think, for instance, of the "Ford Nation" that was brought into being by Toronto's idiosyncratic mayor Rob Ford. Or think of Trump supporters who insist that they are not the *Trumpenproletariat*, as sneering elite critics have claimed, but a group of people with legitimate grievances and ideals that the Republican Party has failed to take seriously. The thought here is similar to John Dewey's insight that publics don't just exist "out there" but are created (one might also remember the Marxist notion that a class needs to become a class for itself—conscious, that is, of being a collective political actor). A well-functioning democracy should be designed to multiply, but also in the end empirically to test, claims to representation.[37] Of course, there is no guarantee that such contestation will actually happen or that struggles for inclusion will be successful. (Or, for that matter, that struggles will be about inclusion in the first place, as opposed to struggles against the constitutional order as such. And, of course, the struggles might also involve claims to *exclusion*.)

Constitutions can ideally facilitate what one might call a "chain of claim-making for inclusion." An initial "We the People" neither entirely disappears inside the regular political process nor stays as an actual, empirical, unified agent—a kind of macrosubject—outside the constituted order. Instead, to whom "We the People" refers remains an open question, one that democracy in many ways is *about*. As Claude Lefort put it, "Democracy inaugurates the experience of an ungraspable, uncontrollable society in which the people will be said to be sovereign, of course, but whose identity will constantly be open to question, whose identity will remain forever latent."[38]

That also means that "the people" is a volatile, risky, maybe outright dangerous expression. Some of the French and American Revolutionaries certainly thought so. Adrien Duquesnoy, in the 1791 edition of *L'Ami des patriotes*, recommended strictly regulating the uses of "people" by citizens.[39] And John Adams made little effort to hide his anxieties about the possible consequences of an uncontrolled usage of "the people": "It is danger- ous to open so fruitful a Source of Controversy and Altercation . . . There would be no End of it. New Claims will arise. Women will demand a Vote. Lads from 12 to 21 will think their Rights not enough attended to, and every Man, who has not a farthing, will demand an Equal Voice, with any other in All Acts of State. It tends to confound and destroy all Distinctions, and prostrate all Ranks, to one common level."[40]

The concept of the people could even be deployed to their own advantage by the very traditional elites that "people power" was supposed to sweep away in democratic revolutions. Bismarck declared in the Reichstag in 1873, "We all belong to the people, I have popular rights [*Volksrechte*], too, to the people also belongs his Majesty the Emperor; we all are the people, not just the gentlemen who are making certain old claims that are traditionally called liberal but are not always liberal. I take exception to them monopolizing the name of the people and to exclude me from the people!"[41]

Democracy makes it possible always to reopen and even to pose with entirely new terms the question of the people, just as it is always possible to criticize the realities of a given democracy in the name of democratic ideals. As Sheldon Wolin once put it, "Democracy was and is the only political ideal that condemns its own denial of equality and inclusion."[42] In that sense, one might also say that democracy suffers from a permanent crisis of representation.[43] And it is important to note that the crisis might not be just about who gets represented but also how citizens get represented, just as the demand for inclusion might turn out to require a change in political and social structures as a whole (as opposed to just including ever more groups into structures that remain essentially unchanged).[44] Democracy as a whole, then, might plausibly have the motto, "Ever tried. Ever failed. No matter. Try again. Fail again. Fail better."

It is actually populists who break off the chain of claim-making by asserting that the people can now be firmly and conclusively identified—and that the people is now actual and no longer latent. It is a kind of final claim. In that sense, populists de facto want a kind of closure (including and especially constitutional closure), quite unlike those who, by arguing for inclusion, should be committed to the idea of further inclusion—or a continuation of the chain of claim-making. Arguably, the Tea Party is a prime example for advocating this kind of constitutional closure.

What about the shouts heard in Tahrir Square—or, going back roughly a quarter century, the emphatic chanting of "We are the People" on the streets of East Germany in the fall of 1989? This slogan is entirely legitimate in the face of a regime that claims exclusively to represent the people but in fact shuts large parts of the people out politically. One could go further and argue that what prima facie might seem like an arch-populist slogan was in fact an antipopulist claim: the regime pretends exclusively to represent the people and their well-considered, long-term interest (or so a standard justification of the "leading role" of state socialist parties went)—but in fact, *das Volk* are something else and want something else. In nondemocracies, "We are the People" is a justified revolutionary claim; it is precisely not a populist one. And in populist regimes that stretch the limits of representative democracy but still retain some respect for procedure (and empirical reality), even a seemingly small contestation of the regime can have enormous repercussions. Think of the single "standing man" on Istanbul's Taksim Square in the wake of the crackdown on the Gezi Park protesters. Demonstrations had been prohibited. But a single man was not demonstrating; he was just standing there, alone—a silent witness, a reminder of Atatürk's republican values (he stood facing Atatürk's statue)—but also a living, literally standing reproach against the government's claim to represent all upright Turks without remainder. He was eventually joined by many standing men and women, none of whom said anything and none of whom held up any messages. Erdoğan in turn remained faithful to one of the governing techniques analyzed earlier in this chapter. His government tried to prove that Erdem Gündüz—that was the name of the "standing man"—was a foreign agent. As Gündüz reported in an interview with a German newspaper, "A journalist close to the government, who later became a consultant for Erdoğan, accused me of being an agent or member of Otpor, the Serbian civic movement, which initiated the fall of Milosevic. And Egemen Bagis, the Minister for European Affairs, tweeted that before my performance I spent three days in the German Embassy. In fact, I have never been to the German Embassy."[45]

Now, whether a particular claim is democratic or populist will not always be a clear-cut, obvious matter. For instance, in Egypt, there was a period between the initial protests on Tahrir Square and the fraught constitution-making process where it was not always easy to discern which was which. (One cannot tell simply by checking whether "the people" are somehow being invoked.) Yet the fact remains that during 2012 and 2013, it became clear that the Muslim Brotherhood was trying to create a populist, partisan constitution that defined its image of the pure people and put in place constraints inspired by their particular understanding of what constitutes a good Egyptian.[46] Confrontation thus became hard to avoid.[47]

How to Deal with Populists

At this stage one might wonder, Why would anyone ever support populists if the latter are so obviously always protoauthoritarians likely to do serious damage to democratic systems? Is the fact that populist leaders have millions of supporters in many countries evidence that these millions have authoritarian personalities (to return to one of the psychological diagnoses discussed in chapter 1)? Are so many of our fellow citizens potentially ready to exclude us, if in their eyes we don't conform to their conception of "real Americans"? In this chapter, I want to make life a little bit more difficult for liberal democrats who by now might be tempted simply to dismiss populism as any kind of challenge at the level of ideas (as opposed to an empirical problem that has to be dealt with one way or another). I shall point to the ways in which the appeal of populism rides on what the Italian democratic theorist Norberto Bobbio used to call the broken promises of democracy. I also want to show how populism seems to solve a problem to which liberal democracy has no real answer—namely, the problem of what should constitute the boundaries of "the people" in the first place. And lastly, I shall try to explain that particular historical circumstances in the

United States and Europe have facilitated an upsurge of populism in our day. I conclude with some suggestions as to how one might best talk *with*—and not just *about*— populists without thereby ending up talking *like* them.

Populism and the Broken Promises of Democracy

What explains the attractiveness of populism? Of course, the beneficiaries of clientelism and discriminatory legalism will find things in it to like. But I would also suggest that the success of populism can be connected to what one might call promises of democracy that have not been fulfilled and that in a certain sense simply can't be fulfilled in our societies. Nobody ever officially issued these promises. They are more like what is sometimes called the "folk theory of democracy"[1]—or intuitions that explain not only democracy's attraction in the modern word but also its periodic failures.

The crucial promise, simply put, is that the people can rule. At least in theory, populists claim that the people as a whole not only have a common and coherent will but also can rule in the sense that the right representatives can implement what the people have demanded in the form of an imperative mandate. Many initial intuitions about democracy can be translated into such a picture: democracy is self-government, and who can rule ideally is not just a majority but the whole. Even in democratic Athens, this story was not the whole story, but Athens came as close as one can imagine to democracy in the sense of cultivating a sense of collective capacity and actually engaging in collective action (but, crucially, on the understanding that citizens would rule and be ruled in turn—there is no democracy without proper rotation into and out of public office).[2] One has to be rather obtuse not to see the attraction of such a notion of collectively mastering one's fate, and one might be forgiven for melancholy feelings given its loss in practice.

Now, populists speak *as if* such promises could be fulfilled. They speak and act *as if* the people could develop a singular judgment, a singular will, and hence a singular, unambiguous mandate. They speak and act *as if* the people were one—with any opposition, if its existence is acknowledged at all, soon to disappear. They speak *as if* the people, if only they empowered the right representatives, could fully master their fate. To be sure, they do not talk about the collective capacity of the people as such, and they do not pretend that the people could actually themselves occupy the offices of the state. As I've been stressing, populism is only thinkable in the context of representative democracy.

The major differences between democracy and populism should have become clear by now: one enables majorities to authorize representatives whose actions may or may not turn out to conform to what a majority of citizens expected or would have wished for; the other pretends that no action of a populist government can be questioned, because "the people" have willed it so. The one assumes fallible, contestable judgments by changing majorities; the other imagines a homogeneous entity outside all institutions whose identity and ideas can be fully represented. The one assumes, if anything, a people of individuals, so that in the end only numbers (in elections) count; the other takes for granted a more or less mysterious "substance" and the fact that even large numbers of individuals (even majorities) can fail to express that substance properly. The one presumes that decisions made after democratic procedures have been followed are not "moral" in such a way that all opposition must be considered immoral; the other postulates one properly moral decision even in circumstances of deep disagreement about morality (and policy). Finally—and most importantly—the one takes it that "the people" can never appear in a noninstitutionalized manner and, in particular, accepts that a majority (and even an "overwhelming majority," a beloved term of Vladimir Putin) in parliament is not "the people" and cannot speak in the name of the people; the other presumes precisely the opposite.

It might seem then that representative democracy can make do without any appeals to "the people." But is that true? Is anything missing at all from such a picture? Or can all legitimate democratic concerns—about increased participation, or better deliberation, or majorities not getting a raw deal in the conditions of contemporary finance capitalism in the West—be rephrased in such a way as to eliminate the need for "the people" entirely?

I think that such concerns can indeed be rephrased—but they might fail to get traction not because "the people" have disappeared but because something else is disappearing before our very eyes: party democracy.[3] Parties once mediated between a pluralist society and a political system that sooner or later had to produce authoritative decisions that would not please everyone. Even "losers" would need to give their consent, albeit secure in the knowledge that there was a reasonable chance that they'd win at some time in the future. Put simply, democracy is a system where you know you can lose, but you also know that you will not always lose. Parties formed governments and legitimate oppositions; their very existence as legitimate "parts" (as opposed to "the whole") had an antipopulist meaning. This was true even of the large "catch-all" parties that called themselves "people's parties," or *Volksparteien*; despite the populist-sounding name, they never claimed exclusively to represent the people as a whole. Rather, they offered two or more competing conceptions of peoplehood, dramatized the differences between them, but also recognized the other side as legitimate. (This approach was particularly attractive in countries that had undergone a civil war but where the need for coexistence was eventually recognized. Think of Austria, where socialist "Reds" and conservative Catholic "Blacks" had to find fair terms of living together in the same political space.) In short, parties represented diversity; party systems symbolized unity.

Today, many indicators suggest that neither parties nor party systems fulfill their respective functions any longer. Scholars have shown that populism is strong in places with weak party systems. Where previously coherent and entrenched party systems broke down, chances for populists clearly increased: just think of how the implosion of the party system in postwar Italy in the early 1990s eventually produced Silvio Berlusconi. If Kelsen was right that democracy under modern conditions can only mean party democracy, then the slow disintegration of parties and party systems is not a tiny empirical detail. It affects the viability of democracy as such, including whatever remains of an ideal of democracy as providing political communities with a sense of unity and collective agency.

Chapter 3

The Liberal Democratic Critique of Populism: Three Problems

So far, I have assumed and even taken for granted that populists go wrong in extracting "the real people" from the empirical totality of the people living in a state and then excluding those citizens who dissent from the populist line. Just think back to George Wallace's incessant talk of "real Americans" or the claim by right-wingers that Barack Obama is an "un-American" or even "anti-American" president. Yet to reproach populists with these exclusions raises a crucial question: What or who decides membership in the people, other than the historical accident of who is born in a particular place or who happens to be the son or daughter of particular parents? Put simply, the charge against populists that they are exclusionary is a normative one, but liberal democrats—unless they advocate for a world state with one single, equal citizenship status—also effectively condone exclusions of all those not part of a particular state. This challenge is known in political theory as the "boundary problem." It famously has no obvious democratic solution: to say that the people should decide presumes that we already know who the people are—but that is the very question that demands an answer.

In fact, we see here a curious reversal. Populists always distinguish morally between those who properly belong and those who don't (even if that moral criterion might ultimately be nothing more than a form of identity politics).[4] Liberal democrats seem only to be able to appeal to the brute facts or, phrased a bit differently, to historical accidents. They can say that *de facto* certain people are also "real Americans" since, after all, they hold American citizenship. But that is indeed just a fact; it does not in and of itself amount to much of a normative claim.

How might we do better here? I suggest two answers. For one thing, criticizing the populists for excluding parts of the people does not require that we *definitively* establish who is and who is not a member of the polity. Nobody has authorized the massive disenfranchisement toward which, at least symbolically, populists gesture. This is not to say that 51 percent of voters officially eliminating the vote of the remaining 49 percent could ever be justified; it is just to point out that many citizens, when confronted with what populists imply, may well respond by saying, "I can criticize certain people in all kinds of ways without actually wanting to deny their status as free and equal fellow citizens." Second, and more important, the boundary problem is not the kind of problem that any political theory *de haut en bas* can solve once and for all. Addressing it is a *process* in which both existing members and aspiring members can have a say; it should be a matter of democratic debate, not a once-and-for-all decision based on unchangeable criteria.[5] It would be a mistake, of course, to think that this process will necessarily mean progress in the sense of more inclusiveness; perhaps, at the end of a genuine democratic debate, definitions of a people will be *more* restrictive than at the beginning.

This is not where the problems end for the liberal democratic critique of populism, though. So far, we have also taken for granted that being an antipluralist is in and of itself undemocratic. Is it? Pluralism—just like its particular variant, multiculturalism—is often presented simultaneously as a fact and as a value. Just like the boundary problem, we're left with the question of why a simple fact should automatically have any moral weight. Then there is the issue that pluralism and diversity are not first-order values as is, for example, freedom. Nobody could plausibly say that more pluralism must automatically always be good. While pluralism and liberalism have often been associated in liberal thought, many philosophers have also rightly insisted that, on closer inspection, it is actually very difficult to get from the presence of pluralism (especially a pluralism of values and lifestyles) to a principled endorsement of liberty.[6] So we need to be much more precise about what's wrong with antipluralism. We might want to say that the real problem with populism is that its denial of diversity effectively amounts to denying the status of certain citizens as free and equal. These citizens might not be excluded officially, but the public legitimacy of their individual values, ideas of what makes for the good life, and even material interests are effectively called into question and even declared not to count. As John Rawls argued, accepting pluralism is not a recognition of the empirical fact that we live in diverse societies; rather, it amounts to a commitment to try to find fair terms of sharing the same political space with others whom we respect as free and equal but also as irreducibly different in their identities and interests. Denying pluralism in this sense amounts to saying, "I can only live in a political world where my conception of the polity, or my personal view of who is a real American, gets to trump all others."[7] This is simply not a democratic perspective on politics.

Finally, there's a concern with how democrats sometimes respond to populist leaders and parties. In a number of countries, the reaction of nonpopulist parties—as well as occasionally the public media—has been to erect a *cordon sanitaire* around populists: no cooperation with them, certainly no political coalitions with them, no debates on TV, and no concessions on any of their policy demands. In some cases, the problems with such strategies of exclusion have been obvious from the start. Nicolas Sarkozy, for instance, kept claiming that the Front National (FN) does not really share basic French republican values; at the same time, he was copying the FN's policies on immigration, making his own party into something like an "FN lite." The evident hypocrisy was bound to undermine any anti-FN strategy. Less obviously, the fact that all political actors other than the populists collude to exclude the latter immediately strengthens the credibility of populists in claiming that the established parties are forming a "cartel"; populists delight in pointing out that their competitors are ultimately all the same, despite their professed ideological differences—hence the tendency to fuse even the names of the established parties to reinforce the sense that only the populists offer a genuine alternative. (In France, for instance, Marine Le Pen used to speak of the "UMPS," fusing the acronym of Sarkozy's right-wing party with that of the socialists.)

Apart from these more practical challenges—which are more about calculating political effects as to what might actually succeed in restraining populist passions—there remains a principled worry. I have insisted that the problem with populists is that they exclude. So what are we supposed to do in return? Exclude them! I have also repeatedly pointed out that populists are committed anti-pluralists. So what do we do by excluding them? Reduce overall pluralism. Something seems not right here. One is reminded of what gave Wallace's counterpunches against liberals such force in his day: he could claim with some plausibility that "the biggest bigots in the world are . . . the ones who call others bigots."[8]

I suggest that, as long as populists stay within the law—and don't incite violence, for instance—other political actors (and members of the media) are under some obligation to engage them. When they enter parliaments, they represent constituents; simply to ignore the populists is bound to reinforce those constituents' sense that "existing elites" have abandoned them or never cared about them in the first place. Yet talking to populists is not the same as talking like populists. One can take their political claims seriously without taking them at face value. In particular, one does not have to accept the ways in which populists frame certain problems. To return to an earlier example, were there really millions of unemployed in France in the 1980s? Yes. Had every single job been taken by an "immigrant," as the Front National wanted the electorate to believe? Of course not.

The point here is not that proper argument and evidence are guaranteed to defeat populists in parliaments, in public debate, and ultimately at the polls. If it is true that populists ultimately appeal to a certain symbolic rendering of the "true people," the appeal of that image will not vanish automatically when voters are presented with some set of correct statistics about a particular policy area. But this doesn't mean that proper argument and evidence cannot make a difference. A significant part of Wallace's support in his 1968 presidential campaign disappeared, for instance, after unions started to bombard their members with information about both the actual situation of "the working man" in Alabama and how little Wallace had done as governor to improve it.[9]

More important still, one can also engage with populists on a symbolic level. This can take the shape of arguing about what a polity's foundational commitments really mean. But it might also come down to the symbolic affirmation of parts of the population that had previously been excluded. As should have become clear, figures like Evo Morales or Erdoğan are not just evil authoritarians who emerged out of nowhere; Morales was justified in advocating for the indigenous peoples of Bolivia who had been largely kept out of the political process, and Erdoğan was doing something democratic when he asserted the presence of what had often been dismissed as "black Turks"—that is to say, the poor and devout Anatolian masses—against the one-sided Westernized image of the Turkish Republic celebrated by the Kemalists. The quest for inclusion did not have to take the form of the *pars pro toto* populist claim; arguably, some of the damage to democracy might have been averted had existing elites been willing to take steps toward both practical *and* symbolic inclusion.

A Crisis of Representation? The American Scene

One of the results of the analysis presented so far—counterintuitive as it might seem—is that the one party in US history that explicitly called itself "populist" was in fact not populist. Populism, as is well known, was a movement primarily of farmers in the 1890s. It briefly threatened the hold of Democrats and Republicans on the US political system. To be sure, it is not the first instance of what historians have seen as populism in American

history. On the one hand, the Founding Fathers themselves were obviously wary of unconstrained popular sovereignty. They precisely tried to avoid a situation
where an imagined collective whole could be played off
against the new political institutions. This is the meaning of the famous words in *Federalist* 63: "It is clear that
the principle of representation was neither unknown to the
ancients nor wholly overlooked in their political constitutions. The true distinction between these and the American
governments, lies IN THE TOTAL EXCLUSION OF THE
PEOPLE, IN THEIR COLLECTIVE CAPACITY, from any
share in the LATTER, and not in the TOTAL EXCLUSION
OF THE REPRESENTATIVES OF THE PEOPLE from the
administration of the FORMER" (emphasis in original).
Still, the Framers also invoked the "genius of the people,"[10]
and the Constitution contained many "popular" elements,
from juries to militias.[11] Thomas Jefferson from the start
provided a republican and producerist language that
would be revived by many political rhetoricians defending the rights of the hardworking majority; virtually all
strands of Protestantism perpetuated the notion that the
people themselves, unaided by clergy, could find spiritual
truth; Andrew Jackson, central to the "Age of the Common Man," with his campaign against the "money power,"
is variously presented as a force for deepening democracy
or as a "populist"—called "King Mob" for a reason—who
created a whole new style of politics in which public figures used references to the "log cabin" and "hard cider"
to demonstrate that they stood with and for the "plain
people." In the 1850s there was the nativist (in particular,
anti-Catholic) Know Nothing movement. It had initially
been called the "Native American Party" before it became

simply the "American Party" (raising a claim to exclusive representation with its very name). Membership was only open to Protestant men and the organization was built on secrecy (hence, when questioned, its adherents were supposed to declare, "I know nothing but my country"). The year 1892 saw the formation of the People's Party, whose adherents were first simply called "Pops"—and, eventually, "Populists." Like so many political labels, this one was initially meant to be derogatory (with "Populites" being another contender for a negative designation) and only later came to be defiantly adopted and celebrated by those whom the name had been meant to denigrate. (The word *neoconservative* had a similar career in the 1970s.)[12]

The self-declared Populists emerged from movements of farmers no longer content to raise corn but determined to raise hell politically. Their experience of debt and dependency—and the economic downturn of the early 1890s in particular—inspired them to organize for a range of demands that variously set them against both the Democrats and the Republicans. In particular, as farmers, they needed cheap credit and transportation to get their produce to the East. Hence they felt increasingly at the mercy of banks and railroad owners. Eventually, their confrontation with what was usually just called "the interests" gave rise to two demands that largely came to define Populism's political program: on the one hand, the creation of a subtreasury—the freeing of silver (against what the "Goldbugs" advocated)—and, on the other, the nationalization of the railroads.[13]

The Populists formulated their demands in political language that clearly set "the people" against self-serving elites. Mary Elizabeth Lease famously stated, "Wall Street owns the country. It is no longer a government of the people, by the people, and for the people, but a government of Wall Street, by Wall Street, and for Wall Street. The great common people of this country are slaves, and monopoly is the master."[14] Populist discourse was suffused with none-too-subtle moral claims; there was talk of "the plutocrats, the aristocrats, and all the other rats"; and some of the slogans (and poetry) are reminiscent of the central tropes of the Occupy Wall Street Movement (for example, the "ninety and nine in hovels bare, the one in a palace with riches rare").[15]

As said above, historians as well as political and social theorists of the 1950s and 1960s often described the Populists as driven by anger and resentment, prone to conspiracy theories, and guilty—not least—of racism. Richard Hofstadter famously spoke of the "paranoid style in American politics."[16] Evidence is not hard to find. Georgia Populist leader Tom Watson once asked, "Did [Jefferson] dream that in 100 years or less *his* party would be prostituted to the vilest purposes of monopoly; that red-eyed Jewish millionaires would be chiefs of that Party, and that the liberty and prosperity of the country would be . . . constantly and corruptly sacrificed to Plutocratic greed in the name of Jeffersonian democracy?"[17] Yet in retrospect, it seems clear that the Cold War liberal historians and political theorists were talking more about McCarthyism and the rise of the radical conservative movement (including its outright racist factions such as the John Birch Society) than the actual Populists of the 1890s.

The Populists were an example of advocacy for the common people—without, I think, pretending to represent the people as a whole. To be sure, there were sometimes ambiguities or (perhaps conscious) slippages, even in the famous Omaha Platform, with which the People's Party had constituted itself:

> We have witnessed for more than a quarter of a century the struggles of the two great political parties for power and plunder, while grievous wrongs have been inflicted upon the suffering people. We charge that the controlling influences dominating both these parties have permitted the existing dreadful conditions to develop without serious effort to prevent or restrain them. Neither do they now promise us any substantial reform. They have agreed together to ignore, in the coming campaign, every issue but one. They propose to drown the outcries of a plundered people with the uproar of a sham battle over the tariff, so that capitalists, corporations, national banks, rings, trusts, watered stock, the demonetization of silver and the oppressions of the usurers may all be lost sight of. They propose to sacrifice our homes, lives, and children on the altar of mammon; to destroy the multitude in order to secure corruption funds from the millionaires.
>
> Assembled on the anniversary of the birthday of the nation, and filled with the spirit of the grand general and chief who established our independence, we seek to restore the government of the Republic to the hands of "the plain people," with which class it originated. We assert our purposes to be identical with the purposes of the National Constitution; to form a more perfect union and establish justice, insure domestic tranquility, provide for the common defence, promote the general welfare, and secure the blessings of liberty for ourselves and our posterity.

The Populists advocated democratic reforms such as the direct election of senators as well as the secret ballot—and they sought graduated taxation and the creation of what today would be called a regulatory state. But they did so with reference to the "plain people." Implementing their ideal of a "cooperative commonwealth" may well have resulted in something that elsewhere in the world would have been called "Social Democracy."[18] As the Omaha Platform made abundantly clear, they respected the Constitution, although in an American context—unlike in a European one—anticonstitutionalism will hardly serve as a useful criterion for identifying populists in the sense defended in this book. After all, the Constitution was and remains revered by virtually everyone.

The Populists rarely ever claimed to be the people as such—although they united men and women, and whites and blacks to a degree that arguably none of the other major parties did at the time. They might have been much more successful had they not been viciously attacked by Southern Democrats in particular: voting fraud and bribery were common, as was violence. Had their demands not been co-opted by both Democrats and Republicans; had they not committed both strategic and tactical errors (over which historians, in a normatively loaded debate, continue to argue today); and had the "Demo-Pop" ticket of William Jennings Bryan, the "the Great Commoner," succeeded in 1896—if all these things had turned out differently, US political history may have taken a very different turn.[19] Yet the Populist movement was not entirely without consequences. After the mid-1890s some Populists went into the Socialist Party; at least some of the main demands of the Populists were realized during the heyday of Progressivism; and, as C. Vann Woodward, in his attack on the misreading of populism by Cold War liberals in the 1950s pointed out, even the New Deal of the 1930s could be said to be a form of "neo-Populism."[20]

None of this is to say that twentieth-century American history has not seen instances of populism in my sense of the term: McCarthyism is an obvious candidate, as would be George Wallace and his followers. Jimmy Carter claimed the label "populist" for himself, but he clearly meant to allude to the Populists of the late nineteenth century (as well as the "populist" associations of evangelical Protestantism and rural and republican—in one word, Jeffersonian—understandings of democracy). In one sense at least, Wallace had paved the way for him: it became imaginable to look to a Southern governor as a source of moral renewal for the United States. (Bill Clinton arguably still benefitted from this legacy of associations nearly two decades later.)

It is with the rise of the Tea Party and Donald Trump's astounding success in 2015–16 that populism as understood in this book has really become of major importance in American politics. Clearly, "anger" has played a role, but as noted earlier, "anger" is not by itself much of an explanation of anything. The reasons for that anger have something to do with a sense that the country is changing culturally in ways deeply objectionable to a certain percentage of American citizens:[21] there is the increasing influence of, broadly speaking, social-sexual liberal values (same-sex marriage, etc.) and also concerns about the United States becoming a "majority-minority country," in which traditional images of "the real people"—white Protestants, that is—have less and less purchase on social reality. In addition to these cultural issues, there are the very real material grievances and, not least, the sense that the economic interests of a significant number of Americans are unrepresented in Washington—an impression that is actually very much confirmed by hard social scientific data.[22]

As Hanspeter Kriesi has argued, Western countries have seen a new conflict line emerge in recent decades—what political scientists call a "cleavage" between citizens who favor more openness and those who prefer some form of closure.[23] This conflict can play out primarily in economic terms, or it can turn into mostly a cultural issue. When identity politics predominates, populists will prosper. The problem is not an economy that less and less fits capitalist self-justifications in terms of competition and heroic entrepreneurship benefiting all. (Even *The Economist*, not exactly a *Marxisant* publication, has begun to criticize monopoly power in the United States.) Instead the issue is said to be Mexicans stealing jobs (and supposedly doing various other things). Now, one should not pretend that all identity issues can seamlessly be translated into questions of material interests; one needs to take individuals' value commitments seriously. It is necessary, however, to remember one important difference between cultural and economic changes: many of the former do not, in the end, directly affect many individuals. People might not like the way the country is going, but who other than wedding photographers with very traditional beliefs about marriage really feel touched in their everyday lives by the legalization of same-sex marriage? It would not be the first time that the United States has developed a more inclusive, tolerant, and generous self-conception as a nation over the objections of a small but passionate faction of voters. A similarly hopeful story cannot be told about the males with no more than a high school diploma whose skills, if any, are simply not needed in the American economy today.

The United States today requires deep structural reform in this respect, and someone like Bernie Sanders clearly is right to draw attention to such a need. As should have become clear by now, Sanders is not a left-wing populist, if one is at all persuaded by the criteria developed in this book. The reason is not that there can't be such a thing as left-wing populism by definition, as some leftists outside the United States sometimes say. Populism isn't about policy content; it's irrelevant that on one level Sanders can sound like Huey Long with his imperative to "Share Our Wealth." Populism is about making a certain kind of moral claim, and the content needed to specify that claim may well come from, for instance, socialist doctrine (Chávez is the obvious example).

Europe between Populism and Technocracy

One implication of the analysis presented in this book is that National Socialism and Italian Fascism need to be understood as populist movements—even though, I hasten to add, they were not just populist movements but also exhibited traits that are not inevitable elements of populism as such: racism, a glorification of violence, and a radical "leadership principle." Now, in Western Europe, one of the peculiarities of the aftermath of the high point of totalitarian politics in the 1930s and 1940s was the following:

both postwar political thought and postwar political institutions were deeply imprinted with antitotalitarianism. Political leaders, as well as jurists and philosophers, sought to build an order designed, above all, to prevent a return to the totalitarian past. They relied on an image of the past as a chaotic era characterized by limitless political dynamism, unbound "masses," and attempts to forge a completely unconstrained political subject—such as the purified German *Volksgemeinschaft* or the "Soviet People" (created in Stalin's image and ratified as real in the "Stalin Constitution" of 1936).

As a consequence, the whole direction of political development in postwar Europe has been toward fragmenting political power (in the sense of checks and balances, or even a mixed constitution) as well as empowering unelected institutions or institutions beyond electoral accountability, such as constitutional courts, all in the name of strengthening democracy itself.[24] That development was based on specific lessons that European elites—rightly or wrongly—drew from the political catastrophes of midcentury: the architects of the postwar Western European order viewed the ideal of popular sovereignty with a great deal of distrust; after all, how could one trust people who had brought fascists to power or extensively collaborated with fascist occupiers? Less obviously, elites also had deep reservations about the idea of parliamentary sovereignty and, more particularly, the idea of political actors claiming to speak and act for the people as a whole being empowered by parliaments (and thereby subscribing to the metapolitical illusion Kelsen had criticized). After all, had not legitimate representative assemblies handed all power over to Hitler and to Marshal Pétain, the leader of

Vichy France, in 1933 and 1940, respectively? Hence parliaments in postwar Europe were systematically weakened, checks and balances strengthened, and institutions without electoral accountability (again, constitutional courts serving as the prime example) tasked not just with defending individual rights but with securing democracy as a whole.[25] In short, distrust of unrestrained popular sovereignty, or even unconstrained *parliamentary* sovereignty (what a German constitutional lawyer once called "parliamentary absolutism") are, so to speak, built into the DNA of postwar European politics. These underlying principles of what I have elsewhere called "constrained democracy" were almost always adopted when countries were able to shake off dictatorships and turn to liberal democracy in the last third of the twentieth century—first on the Iberian peninsula in the 1970s and then in Central and Eastern Europe after 1989.

European integration, it needs to be emphasized, was part and parcel of this comprehensive attempt to constrain the popular will: it added supranational constraints to national ones.[26] (Which is not to say that this entire process was masterminded by anyone, or came about seamlessly. Of course, the outcomes were contingent and had to do with who prevailed in particular political struggles—a point that is particularly clear in the case of individual rights protection, a role for which national courts and the European Court of Justice competed.) This logic was more evident initially with institutions like the Council of Europe and the European Convention on Human Rights. But the desire to "lock in" liberal-democratic commitments became more pronounced in the specific case of the European Union (EU; or, as it was known until 1993, the European Economic Community [EEC]) context with the transitions to democracy in Southern Europe in the 1970s.

Now, the upshot of this brief historical excursus is that a political order built on a distrust of popular sovereignty—an explicitly antitotalitarian and, if you like, implicitly antipopulist order—will always be particularly vulnerable to political actors speaking in the name of the people as a whole against a system that appears designed to minimize popular participation. As should have become clear from the discussion in this book, populism is actually not really a cry for more political participation, let alone for the realization of direct democracy. But it can resemble movements making such cries and hence, prima facie, gain some legitimacy on the grounds that the postwar European order really *is* based on the idea of keeping "the people" at a distance.

Why might Europe have become particularly vulnerable to populist actors since the mid-1970s or so, and in recent years in particular? Some answers might seem obvious: a retrenchment of the welfare state, immigration, and, above all in recent years, the Eurocrisis. But a crisis—whether economic, social, or ultimately also political—does not automatically produce populism in the sense defended in this book (except, possibly, when old party systems are disintegrating). On the contrary, democracies can be said perpetually to create crises and, at the same time, to have the resources and mechanisms for self-correction.[27] Rather, at least as far as the current wave of populism in Europe is concerned, I would say that it is the particular approach to addressing the Eurocrisis—for shorthand, technocracy—that is crucial for understanding the present-day rise of populism.

In a curious way, the two mirror each other. Technocracy holds that there is only one correct policy solution; populism claims that there is only one authentic will of the people.[28] Most recently, they have also been trading attributes: technocracy has become moralized ("you Greeks, and so on, must atone for your sins!"—that is, profligacy in the past), whereas populism has become businesslike (think of Berlusconi and, in the Czech Republic, Babiš' promise to run the state like one of his companies). For neither technocrats nor populists is there any need for democratic debate. In a sense, both are curiously apolitical. Hence it is plausible to assume that one might pave the way for the other, because each legitimizes the belief that there is no real room for disagreement. After all, each holds that there is only one correct policy solution and only one authentic popular will respectively.

Noting this parallel allows us to see a bit more clearly what really separates populist parties and movements on the one hand from actors who, on the other hand, might oppose, say, austerity measures and libertarian economic prescriptions while not resembling populists in any other sense. In Finland, the thing that makes the party of "True Finns" (and, more recently, just "The Finns") a populist party is not that they criticize the EU but that they claim exclusively to represent true Finns. In Italy, it is not Beppe Grillo's complaints about Italy's *la casta* that should lead one to worry about him as a populist but his assertion that his movement wants (and deserves) nothing less than 100 percent of the seats in parliament, because all other contenders are supposedly corrupt and immoral. According to this logic, the *grillini* ultimately are the pure Italian people—which then also justifies the kind of dictatorship of virtue inside the Five Star Movement that I touched on earlier.

Identifying actual populists and distinguishing them from political actors who criticize elites but do not employ a *pars pro toto* logic (such as the *indignados* in Spain) is a prime task for a theory of populism in Europe today. What some observers have called "democratic activists"—as opposed to populists—first of all advance particular policies, but to the extent that they use people-talk at all, their claim is not "We, and only we, are the people"; it is rather "We are also the people."[29]

It is also important to sow some doubt about left-wing strategies that attempt selectively to draw on the populist imaginary to oppose a neoliberal hegemony. The point is not that critique of the latter is somehow in and of itself populist (in line with the understanding of populism as a matter of "irresponsible policies"). Rather, the trouble is with schemes—very much inspired, it seems, by Ernesto Laclau's maxim that "constructing a people is the main task of radical politics"—that aim to portray today's main political conflict as one between the people (the "governed") on the one hand and the "market people," the de facto governors in the form of investment managers, on the other.[30] Will such an opposition actually mobilize "the people"? Unlikely. Will it import the problems of a genuinely populist conception of politics? Possibly.

Hence the demand for a specific "left-wing populism" to oppose austerity policies (or, for that matter, to counter the rise of right-wing populism) in many parts of Europe is either redundant or dangerous. It is redundant if the point is simply to offer a credible left-wing alternative or a reinvented Social Democracy. Why not talk about building new majorities instead of gesturing at the "construction of a people"? What people exactly? However, if left-wing populism really means *populism* in the sense defined and defended in this book, it is clearly dangerous.

What is the alternative? An approach that seeks to bring in those currently excluded—what some sociologists sometimes call "the superfluous"—while also keeping the very wealthy and powerful from opting out of the system. This is really just another way of saying that some sort of new social contract is needed. Broad-based support is required for such a new social contract in Southern European countries, and that support can only be built through an appeal to fairness, not just fiscal rectitude. To be sure, lofty appeals are not enough; there has to be a mechanism to authorize such a new settlement. It might come in the shape of a grand coalition actually empowered at election time. Alternatively, societies could officially renegotiate their very constitutional settlements, as Iceland and, in a much less dramatic way, Ireland have been trying to do, albeit without much success.

Conclusion

Seven Theses on Populism

1. Populism is neither the authentic part of modern democratic politics nor a kind of pathology caused by irrational citizens. It is the permanent shadow of representative politics. There is always the possibility for an actor to speak in the name of the "real people" as a way of contesting currently powerful elites. There was no populism in ancient Athens; demagoguery perhaps, but no populism, since the latter exists only in representative systems. Populists are not against the principle of political representation; they just insist that only they themselves are legitimate representatives.

2. Not everyone who criticizes elites is a populist. In addition to being antielitist, populists are antipluralist. They claim that they and they alone represent the people. All other political competitors are essentially illegitimate, and anyone who does not support them is not properly part of the people. When in opposition, populists will necessarily insist that elites are immoral, whereas the people are a moral, homogeneous entity whose will cannot err.

3. It can often seem that populists claim to represent the common good as willed by the people. On closer inspection, it turns out that what matters for populists is less the product of a genuine process of will-formation or a common good that anyone with common sense can glean than a symbolic representation of the "real people" from which the correct policy is then deduced. This renders the political position of a populist immune to empirical refutation. Populists can always play off the "real people" or "silent majority" against elected representatives and the official outcome of a vote.

4. While populists often call for referenda, such exercises are not about initiating open-ended processes of democratic will-formation among citizens. Populists simply wish to be confirmed in what they have already determined the will of the real people to be. Populism is not a path to more participation in politics.

5. Populists can govern, and they are likely to do so in line with their basic commitment to the idea that only they represent the people. Concretely, they will engage in occupying the state, mass clientelism and corruption, and the suppression of anything like a critical civil society. These practices find an explicit moral justification in the populist political imagination and hence can be avowed openly. Populists can also write constitutions; these will be partisan or "exclusive" constitutions designed to keep populists in power in the name of perpetuating some supposed original and authentic popular will. They are likely to lead to serious constitutional conflict at some point or other.

6. Populists should be criticized for what they are—a real danger to democracy (and not just to "liberalism"). But that does not mean that one should not engage them in political debate. Talking with populists is not the same as talking like populists. One can take the problems they raise seriously without accepting the ways in which they frame these problems.

7. Populism is not a corrective to liberal democracy in the sense of bringing politics "closer to the people" or even reasserting popular sovereignty, as is sometimes claimed. But it can be useful in making it clear that parts of the population really are unrepresented (the lack of representation might concern interests or identity, or both). This does not justify the populist claim that only their supporters are the real people and that they are the sole legitimate representatives. Populism, then, should force defenders of liberal democracy to think harder about what current failures of representation might be. It should also push them to address more general moral questions. What are the criteria for belonging to the polity? Why exactly is pluralism worth preserving? And how can one address the concerns of populist voters understood as free and equal citizens, not as pathological cases of men and women driven by frustration, anger, and resentment? The hope is that this book has suggested at least some preliminary answers to these questions.

Notes

Introduction

1 Ivan Krastev, "The Populist Moment," available at http://www.eurozine.com/articles/2007-09-18-krastev-en.html, accessed March 1, 2012.

2 Daniel A. Bell, *The China Model: Political Meritocracy and the Limits of Democracy* (Princeton, NJ: Princeton University Press, 2015).

Chapter 1

1 Ghita Ionescu and Ernest Gellner, "Introduction," in Ghita Ionescu and Ernest Gellner (eds.), *Populism: Its Meaning and National Character* (London: Weidenfeld & Nicolson, 1969), 1–5; here 1.

2 For a systematic treatment of the dilemma for governments to be responsible or responsive, see Peter Mair, *Ruling the Void: The Hollowing of Western Democracy* (New York: Verso, 2013).

3 Cas Mudde and Cristóbal Rovira Kaltwasser (eds.), *Populism in Europe and the Americas: Threat or Corrective for Democracy?* (New York: Cambridge University Press, 2013).

4 Benjamin Arditi, "Populism as an Internal Periphery of Democratic Politics," in Francisco Panizza (ed.), *Populism and the Mirror of Democracy* (London: Verso, 2005), 72–98.

5 To be sure, a certain kind of populism in the name of liberal values has become prominent in some European countries in recent years. Think of Pim Fortuyn and Geert Wilders in the Netherlands. But this is still populism that employs "freedom" and "tolerance" as markers of moral difference to distinguish a proper people from others who do not belong; it is not liberalism.

6 Which is not to say that all is relative. Democracy is a highly contested concept as well, but that is no reason to give up on doing democratic theory.

7 Technically speaking, I am trying to construct an ideal type in the sense suggested by Max Weber. The purpose of doing so is partly to bring out what I consider crucial differences between populism and democracy. The obvious danger here is one of circularity: one builds characteristics one finds politically, morally, or even aesthetically distasteful into one's definition of populism only to find that populism and democracy are different—an operation made easier if one can pretend that democracy is not itself a contested concept but has a meaning on which all must agree. Put differently, there is the peril of getting a very clear-cut normative picture only by painting contrasts in a highly partisan way. Which is not the same worry as that of scholars in comparative politics working on populism; their prime anxiety is conceptual stretching. See Giovanni Sartori, "Concept Misformation in Comparative Politics," in *American Political Science Review*, vol. 64 (1970), 1033–53.

8 I share a concern about what one might call "theory theory"—the kind of political theory that is mainly concerned with responding to other theories, as opposed to an engagement with contemporary history in all its complexity and, often, sheer opaqueness. But I do not think that such a concern is best expressed through histrionic calls for "realism," which can only give rise to more theory theory, just this time about a reified "realism." Rather than debating whether "What is to be done?" is a legitimate question, theorists should do something.

9 Ralf Dahrendorf, "Acht Anmerkungen zum Populismus," in *Transit: Europäische Revue*, no. 25 (2003), 156–63.

10 There is the separate issue that neoliberal policy content and populism—as a logic of claims—can perfectly well go together. See Kurt Weyland, "Neopopulism and Neoliberalism in Latin America:

Unexpected Affinities," in *Studies in Comparative International Development*, vol. 31 (1996), 3–31; and Cristóbal Rovira Kaltwasser, "From Right Populism in the 1990s to Left Populism in the 2000s—And Back Again?," in Juan Pablo Luna and Cristóbal Rovira Kaltwasser (eds.), *The Resilience of the Latin American Right* (Baltimore: Johns Hopkins University Press, 2014), 143–66.

11 A question any *responsible* reader of Max Weber would surely ask immediately.

12 Karin Priester, *Rechter und linker Populismus: Annäherung an ein Chamäleon* (Frankfurt am Main: Campus, 2012), 17.

13 On this "gender gap," see Cas Mudde and Cristóbal Rovira Kaltwasser, "Populism," in Michael Freeden et al. (eds.), *The Oxford Handbook of Political Ideologies* (New York: Oxford University Press, 2013), S. 493–512.

14 Vanessa Williamson, Theda Skocpol, and John Coggin, "The Tea Party and the Remaking of Republican Conservatism," in *Perspectives on Politics*, vol. 9 (2011), 25–43; here 33.

15 Mark Elchardus and Bram Spruyt, "Populism, Persistent Republicanism and Declinism: An Empirical Analysis of Populism as a Thin Ideology," in *Government and Opposition*, vol. 51 (2016), 111–33.

16 Roy Kemmers, Jeroen van der Waal, and Stef Aupers, "Becoming Politically Discontented: Anti-Establishment Careers of Dutch Non-voters and PVV Voters," in *Current Sociology*, http://csi.sagepub.com/content/early/2015/11/15/0011392115609651.full.pdf+html.

17 It is worth pointing out that one cannot be resentful and angry at the same time: anger will express itself immediately; resentment will "fester" as a longing for revenge grows over time.

18 Max Scheler, *Ressentiment*, ed. Lewis A. Coser, trans. William W. Holdheim (New York: Free Press, 1961).

19 Bert N. Bakker, Matthijs Rooduijn, and Gijs Schumacher, "The Psychological Roots of Populist Voting: Evidence from the United States, the Netherlands and Germany," in *European Journal of Political Research*, vol. 55 (2016), 302–20. The authors of this study conclude unashamedly: "Populists like Marin Le Pen, Geert Wilders, Sarah Palin and Nigel Farage have mastered the skill of activating voters with low agreeable personalities. That is what unites them *across* political contexts, what separates them from existing parties *within* political contexts, and what underlies their perhaps unexpected success" (317).

20 For an account of how emotions have "cognitive antecedents," see Jon Elster, *Alchemies of the Mind: Rationality and the Emotions* (Cambridge: Cambridge University Press, 1999).

21 It does not follow, however, that everyone criticized as "populist" today is normatively validated as a proper radical democrat, as Marco D'Eramo seems to think. See his "Populism and the New Oligarchy," in *New Left Review*, no. 82 (July–August 2013), 5–28.

22 Seymour M. Lipset, *Political Man: The Social Bases of Politics* (Garden City, NY: Doubleday, 1963), 178.

23 Victor C. Ferkiss, "Populist Influences on American Fascism," in *The Western Political Quarterly*, vol. 10 (1957), 350–73; here 352.

24 For an attempt to go beyond simplistic diagnoses of resentment in the case of the Tea Party, see Lisa Disch, "The Tea Party: A 'White Citizenship Movement?,'" in Lawrence Rosenthal and Christine Trost (eds.), *Steep: The Precipitous Rise of the Tea Party* (Berkeley: University of California Press, 2012), 133–51.

25 Helmut Dubiel, "Das Gespenst des Populismus," in Helmut Dubiel (ed.), *Populismus und Aufklärung* (Frankfurt am Main: Suhrkamp. 1986), 33–50; here 35.

26 As I shall argue later, populists are not against representation—hence I disagree with analyses that pit "populist democracy" against "representative democracy"; for example, see the otherwise excellent article by Koen Abts and Stefan Rummens, "Populism versus Democracy," in *Political Studies*, vol. 55 (2007), 405–24.

27 There is some empirical evidence that voters of populist parties also espouse distinctly intolerant and antipluralist views. See Agnes Akkerman, Cas Mudde, and Andrej Zaslove, "How Populist Are the People? Measuring Populist Attitudes in Voters," in *Comparative Political Studies* (2013), 1–30.

28 Claude Lefort, *Democracy and Political Theory*, trans. David Macey (Cambridge, UK: Polity, 1988), 79.

29 Nancy L. Rosenblum, *On the Side of the Angels: An Appreciation of Parties and Partisanship* (Princeton, NJ: Princeton University Press, 2008).

30 See also C. Vann Woodward, "The Populist Heritage and the Intellectual," in *The American Scholar*, vol. 29 (1959–60), 55–72.

31 Andrew Arato, "Political Theology and Populism," in *Social Research*, vol. 80 (2013), 143–72.

32 "The Inaugural Address of Governor George C. Wallace, January 14, 1963, Montgomery, Alabama," available at http://digital.archives .alabama.gov/cdm/ref/collection/voices/id/2952, accessed April 28, 2016.

33 Wallace made this equation of the real United States with "Southland" very explicit when he argued: "Hear me Southerners! You sons and daughters who have moved north and west throughout this nation . . . we call on you from your native soil to join with us in national support and vote . . . and we know . . . wherever you are . . . away from the hearts of Southland . . . that you will respond, for though you may live in the fartherest reaches of this vast country . . . your heart has never left Dixieland." See ibid.

34 Ibid.

35 I am grateful to Damon Linker for pointing me to this quote. See "CBS Weekend News," *Internet Archive*, May 7, 2016, https://archive.org/ details/KPIX_20160508_003000_CBS_Weekend_News#start/540/ end/600.

36 Margaret Canovan, *The People* (Cambridge, UK: Polity, 2005).

37 Producerism cannot be purely economic—it is a moral concept valorizing the producers. Think of Georges Sorel's political thought as a primary example.

38 Michael Kazin, *The Populist Persuasion: An American History* (Ithaca, NY: Cornell University Press, 1998).

39 We know have the benefit of a whole academic literature on the meaning of "natural-born citizen." See, for instance, Paul Clement and Neal Katyal, "On the Meaning of 'Natural Born Citizen,'" in *Harvard Law Review*, March 11, 2016, http://harvardlawreview.org/2015/03/ on-the-meaning-of-natural-born-citizen.

40 I am grateful to Ivan Krastev and Zsolt Enyedi in this context.

41 Here populists can all of a sudden sound like defenders of epistemic conceptions of democracy.

42 Cas Mudde and Cristóbal Rovira Kaltwasser, "Populism," in Michael Freeden et al. (eds.), *The Oxford Handbook of Political Ideologies* (New York: Oxford University Press, 2013), 493–512.

43 Pierre Rosanvallon has argued that populism involves a *triple* simplification: first, a political-sociological simplification along the lines of homogeneous people versus corrupt elites; second, a procedural and institutional simplification directed against the messy world of intermediary powers; and third, a simplification of the social bond

that is reduced to being a matter of homogeneous identity. See Pierre Rosanvallon, "Penser le populisme," in *La Vie des idées*, September 27, 2011, available at http://www.laviedesidees.fr/Penser-le-populisme.html, accessed February 18, 2016.

44 Quoted in Zsolt Enyedi, "Plebeians, *Citoyens* and Aristocrats, or Where Is the Bottom of the Bottom-up? The Case of Hungary," in Hanspeter Kriesi and Takis S. Pappas (eds.), *European Populism in the Shadow of the Great Recession* (Colchester, UK: ECPR Press, 2015), 235–50; here 239–40.

45 As Jill Lepore has pointed out, the term used to be a euphemism for the dead, until Nixon used it to refer to a supposed majority supporting the Vietnam War. Jill Lepore, *The Whites of Their Eyes: The Tea Party's Revolution and the Battle over American History* (Princeton, NJ: Princeton University Press, 2010), 4–5.

46 See, for instance, Giovanni Gentile, "The Philosophic Basis of Fascism," in *Foreign Affairs*, vol. 6 (1927–28), 290–304.

47 Hans Kelsen, *Vom Wesen und Wert der Demokratie* (1929; repr., Aalen: Scientia, 1981), 22. Kelsen also concluded that modern democracy inevitably had to be party democracy.

48 The populist symbolic image of the people is not something entirely novel. A medieval theorist like Baldus held a conception, analogous to the theory of the king's two bodies, according to which there was the empirical, ever-changing people as a group of individuals on the one hand—and, on the other, the eternal *populus* as a *corpus mysticum*. See Ernst H. Kantorowicz, *The King's Two Bodies: A Study in Medieval Political Theology* (1957; repr., Princeton, NJ: Princeton University Press, 1997), 209. The *corpus mysticum* had corporational character signifying a fictitious or juristic (collective) person; hence it was used synonymously with *corpus fictum*, *corpus imaginatum*, and *corpus repraesentatum*. Just as there was always a possibility of distinguishing the king body politic from the king body natural, so the people body politic (what Baldus called *hominum collection in unum corpus mysticum*) and the people as represented and mediated via institutions could be separated. And just as it was not a paradox, then, for the opponents of Charles I to "fight the king to defend the king," populists claim to fight democratically elected elites to defend the true people and thus democracy. The king's two bodies appear alive and well when a follower of Chávez explains,

"To tell us Chavistas that Chávez is dead is like telling Christians that Christ is dead." See Carl Moses, "Bildersturm in Caracas," in *Frankfurter Allgemeine Zeitung*, January 8, 2016, http://www.faz.net/aktuell/politik/ausland/amerika/venezuela-bildersturm-in-caracas-14004250-p2.html?printPagedArticle=true#pageIndex_2, accessed January 15, 2016.

49 Pierre Rosanvallon, "Revolutionary Democracy," in Pierre Rosanvallon, *Democracy Past and Future*, ed. Samuel Moyn (New York: Columbia University Press, 2006), 79–97; here 79–82. John Quincy Adams observed once: "Democracy has no monuments. It strikes no medals. It bears the head of no man on a coin. Its very essence is iconoclastic." Quoted in Jason Frank, "The Living Image of the People," in *Theory & Event*, vol. 18, no. 1 (2015), at https://muse.jhu.edu/article/566086. In fact, there were statues of democracy in predemocratic times, often in plain clothes and holding snakes (symbolizing that the people were confined to the ground—and, one would think, potentially poisonous). See Uwe Fleckner et al. (eds.), *Politische Ikonographie: Ein Handbuch* (Munich: C. H. Beck, 2011).

50 See, for instance, the SVP's "contract," available at http://www.svp.ch/de/assets/File/positionen/vertrag/Vertrag.pdf, accessed February 13, 2015.

51 Christopher H. Achen and Larry M. Bartels, *Democracy for Realists: Why Elections Do Not Produce Responsive Government* (Princeton, NJ: Princeton University Press, 2016).

52 Quoted in Paula Diehl, "The Populist Twist," manuscript on file with author.

53 Kathleen Bruhn, "'To Hell with Your Corrupt Institutions!': AMLO and Populism in Mexico," in Cas Mudde and Cristóbal Rovira Kaltwasser (eds.), *Populism in Europe and the Americas: Threat or Corrective for Democracy?* (New York: Cambridge University Press, 2012), 88–112.

54 Mark Meckler and Jenny Beth Martin, *Tea Party Patriots: The Second American Revolution* (New York: Holt, 2012), 14.

55 Bernard Manin, *The Principles of Representative Government* (New York: Cambridge University Press, 1997).

56 Ibid.

57 Ibid. "Identity" actually was the promise of a movement like National Socialism, legally operationalized by Carl Schmitt to emphasize the crucial role of *Artgleichheit*, the racial homogeneity or identity

between the Führer and the people. See Carl Schmitt, *Staat, Bewegung, Volk: Die Dreigliederung der politischen Einheit* (Hamburg: Hanseatische Verlagsgesellschaft, 1935).

58 Nadia Urbinati, "A Revolt against Intermediary Bodies," in *Constellations*, vol. 22 (2015), 477–86; and Nadia Urbinati, "Zwischen allgemeiner Anerkennung und Misstrauen," in *Transit: Europäische Revue*, no. 44 (2013).

59 Quoted in Diehl, "Populist Twist."

60 Beppe Grillo, Gianroberto Casaleggio, and Dario Fo, *5 Sterne: Über Demokratie, Italien und die Zukunft Europas*, trans. Christine Ammann, Antje Peter, and Walter Kögler (Stuttgart: Klett-Cotta, 2013), 107.

61 Jonathan White and Lea Ypi, "On Partisan Political Justification," in *American Political Science Review*, vol. 105 (2011), 381–96.

62 Paul Lucardie and Gerrit Voerman, "Geert Wilders and the Party for Freedom in the Netherlands: A Political Entrepreneur in the Polder," in Karsten Grabow and Florian Hartleb (eds.), *Exposing the Demagogues: Right-Wing and National Populist Parties in Europe*, 187–203, http://www.kas.de/wf/doc/kas_35420-544-2-30.pdf?140519123322, accessed January 15, 2016. To be sure, Wilders's complete control also had pragmatic reasons: he had witnessed how the party of Pim Fortuyn completely disintegrated after Fortuyn had been assassinated in May 2002. See Sarah L. de Lange and David Art, "Fortuyn versus Wilders: An Agency-Based Approach to Radical Right Party Building," in *West European Politics*, vol. 34 (2011), 1229–49.

63 De Lange and Art, "Fortuyn versus Wilders," 1229–49.

64 Diehl, "Populist Twist."

65 In actual fact, the Lega Nord was organized like a clan, while the Front National was led by one family (Jean-Marie Le Pen was succeeded by his daughter Marine; Marine now in turn is building up her niece Marion. Currently, six members of the Le Pen family serve as party candidates). See Ulrike Guérot, "Marine Le Pen und die Metmorphose der französischen Republik," in *Leviathan*, vol. 43 (2015), 139–74.

66 Michael Saward, "The Representative Claim," in *Contemporary Political Theory*, vol. 5 (2006), 297–318.

67 Ibid., 298.

68 Paulina Ochoa-Espejo, "Power to Whom? The People between Procedure and Populism," in Carlos de la Torre (ed.), *The Promise and*

Perils of Populism: Global Perspectives (Lexington: University Press of Kentucky, 2015), 59–90.

69 Rosenblum, *On the Side of the Angels.*

70 Jürgen Habermas, *Faktizität und Geltung: Beiträge zur Diskustheorie des Rechts und des demokratischen Rechtsstaats* (Frankfurt am Main: Suhrkamp, 1994), 607.

71 Benjamin Moffitt and Simon Tormey, "Rethinking Populism: Politics, Mediatisation and Political Style," in *Political Studies*, vol. 62 (2014), 381–97.

72 Robert S. Jansen, "Populist Mobilization: A New Theoretical Approach to Populism," in *Sociological Theory*, vol. 29 (2011), 75–96.

73 See Keith Hawkins, "Is Chávez Populist? Measuring Populist Discourse in Comparative Perspective," in *Comparative Political Studies*, vol. 42 (2009), 1040–67; and more broadly the work of "Team Populism," available at https://populism.byu.edu/Pages/Home.aspx, accessed April 22, 2016.

Chapter 2

1 A useful exception is Daniele Albertazzi and Duncan McDonnell, *Populists in Power* (New York: Routledge, 2015).

2 José Pedro Zúquete, "The Missionary Politics of Hugo Chávez," in *Latin American Politics and Society*, vol. 50 (2008), 91–121; here 105.

3 Benjamin Moffitt, "How to Perform Crisis: A Model for Understanding the Key Role of Crisis in Contemporary Populism," in *Government and Opposition*, vol. 50 (2015), 189–217.

4 Carlos de la Torre, *Populist Seduction in Latin America* (Athens: Ohio University Press, 2010), 188.

5 Which is not to say that all these leaders are exactly the same in style or substance. Especially Morales has attempted an inclusionary approach, not least in drafting a new constitution for Bolivia. His "committed constitutionalism" offered many new basic rights (including the right to the good life and rights for nature itself); Morales also sought to recognize previously excluded minorities by declaring Bolivia a "plurinational" state.

6 Bernard Manin, *The Principles of Representative Government* (New York: Cambridge University Press, 1997); and Jeffrey Edward

Green, *The Eyes of the People: Democracy in an Age of Spectatorship* (New York: Oxford University Press, 2010).

7 For the argument that mass clientelism was an early form of democracy, see Francis Fukuyama, *Political Order and Political Decay* (New York: FSG, 2014).

8 See Kurt Weyland, "The Threat from the Populist Left," in *Journal of Democracy*, vol. 24 (2013), 18–32.

9 For the Venezuelan case, see Sebastián L. Mazzuca, "The Rise of Rentier Populism," in *Journal of Democracy*, vol. 24 (2013), 108–22.

10 See Yolanda Valery, "Boliburguesía: Nueva clase venezolana," http://www.bbc.com/mundo/economia/2009/12/091202_1045_venezuela _boliburguesia_wbm.shtml, accessed January 15, 2016.

11 Populist regimes constantly work on formatting societies in a particular image. Orbán created an Orwellian-sounding "System of National Cooperation"; Erdoğan steadily admonishes Turks that everyone in society has to know their proper place (and their limits). See H. Ertuğ Tombuş, "Erdoğan's Turkey: Beyond Legitimacy and Legality," http://researchturkey.org/erdogans-turkey-beyond-legitimacy-and-legality, accessed January 15, 2016.

12 Karin Priester, *Rechter und linker Populismus: Annäherung an ein Chamäleon* (Frankfurt am Main: Campus, 2012), 20.

13 Carl Schmitt, *The Crisis of Parliamentary Democracy*, trans. Ellen Kennedy (Cambridge, MA: MIT Press, 1988), 16–17.

14 See "Viktor Orbán's Speech at the 14th Kötcse Civil Picnic," http://www.kormany.hu/en/the-prime-minister/the-prime-minister -s-speeches/viktor-orban-s-speech-at-the-14th-kotcse-civil-picnic, accessed January 15, 2016.

15 Wolfgang Merkel et al. (eds.), *Defekte Demokratien*, 2 vols. (Opladen: Leske + Budrich, 2003).

16 An illuminating exception is the FLJS policy brief by Cristóbal Rovira Kaltwaser, *Populism vs. Constitutionalism?*, http://www.fljs.org/ sites/www.fljs.org/files/publications/Kaltwasser.pdf, accessed June 16, 2015.

17 For this critique, see also: Corey Brettschneider, "Popular Constitutionalism Contra Populism," in *Constitutional Commentary*, vol. 30 (2015), 81–88. The main reference point for debates about popular constitutionalism in the United States remains Larry Kramer's *The People Themselves* (New York: Oxford University Press, 2004).

18 Witness, for instance, Elizabeth Beaumont writing, "I take the liberty of using the terms civic and popular loosely and interchangeably as laymen's terms meaning largely ordinary people, citizens, or nonofficial," in *The Civic Constitution: Civic Visions and Struggles in the Path toward Constitutional Democracy* (New York: Oxford University Press, 2011l4), 4. Or think of Tom Donnelly claiming that for all their differences, advocates of popular constitutionalism share a "populist sensibility"—which comes down to nothing more than "a common belief that the American people (and their elected representatives) should play an ongoing role in shaping contemporary constitutional meaning." Tom Donnelly, "Making Popular Constitutionalism Work," in *Wisconsin Law Review* (2012), 159–94; here 161–62.

19 Richard D. Parker, "'Here the People Rule': A Constitutional Populist Manifesto," in *Valparaiso University Law Review*, vol. 27 (1993), 531–84; here 532.

20 Martin Loughlin, "The Constitutional Imagination," in *Modern Law Review*, vol. 78 (2015), 1–25.

21 Bruce Ackerman, "Three Paths to Constitutionalism—And the Crisis of the European Union," in *British Journal of Political Science*, vol. 45 (2015), 705–14.

22 For the notion of a façade constitution, see Giovanni Sartori, "Constitutionalism: A Preliminary Discussion," in *American Political Science Review*, vol. 56 (1962), 853–64.

23 Dan Edelstein, *The Terror of Natural Right: Republicanism, the Cult of Nature, and the French Revolution* (Chicago: University of Chicago Press, 2009).

24 Renáta Uitz, "Can You Tell When an Illiberal Democracy Is in the Making? An Appeal to Comparative Constitutional Scholarship from Hungary," in *International Journal of Constitutional Law*, vol. 13 (2015), 279–300; here 286. On the new Hungarian constitution, see also the special section on Hungary's illiberal turn in the *Journal of Democracy*, vol. 23 (2012) and the collection edited by Gábor Attila Tóth, *Constitution for a Disunited Nation: On Hungary's 2011 Fundamental Law* (Budapest: CEU Press, 2012).

25 Quoted in Agnes Batory, "Populists in Government? Hungary's 'System of National Cooperation,'" in *Democratization*, vol. 23 (2016), 283–303.

26 Uitz, "Can You Tell When an Illiberal Democracy Is in the Making?"

27 Dieter Grimm, "Types of Constitutions," in Michel Rosenfeld and András Sajó (eds.), *The Oxford Handbook of Comparative Constitutional Law* (New York: Oxford University Press, 2012), 98–132.

28 See, in particular, the works of Roberto Viciano Pastor and Rubén Martínez Dalmau. The earlier case of Colombia is less obviously a case of what sympathetic observers have called *nuevo constitucionalismo latinoamericano.*

29 David Landau, "Abusive Constitutionalism," in *University of California Davis Law Review*, vol. 47 (2013), 189–260; here 213.

30 "Ein Schritt in Richtung Demokratie," in *Frankfurter Allgemeine Zeitung*, January 5, 2016, http://www.faz.net/aktuell/politik/ausland/amerika/parlament-in-venezuela-tritt-mit-oppositioneller-mehrheit-zusammen-13999306.html, accessed 15 January 2016.

31 Ibid.

32 Bryan Garsten, "Representative Government and Popular Sovereignty," in Ian Shapiro, Susan C. Stokes, Elisabeth Jean Wood, and Alexander S. Kirshner (eds.), *Political Representation* (New York: Cambridge University Press, 2009), 90–110; here 91.

33 Christoph Möllers, *Demokratie: Zumutungen und Versprechen* (Berlin: Wagenbach, 2008), 33–34.

34 Gilbert Achcar, *The People Want: A Radical Exploration of the Arab Uprising* (Berkeley: University of California Press, 2013), 1.

35 Ernesto Laclau, *On Populist Reason* (London: Verso, 2005). Laclau claims that "it is easy . . . to see that the condition of possibility of the political and the conditions of possibility of populism are the same: they both presuppose social division; in both we find an ambiguous *demos* which is, on the one hand, a section within the community (an underdog) and, on the other hand, an agent presenting itself, in antagonistic way, as *the whole* community." See his "Populism: What's in a Name?," in *Populism and the Mirror of Democracy* (London: Verso, 2005), 32–49; here 48.

36 For the following, see Jason Frank, *Constituent Moments: Enacting the People in Postrevolutionary America* (Durham: Duke University Press, 2010).

37 Garsten, "Representative Government."

38 Claude Lefort, *The Political Forms of Modern Society: Bureaucracy, Democracy, Totalitarianism*, ed. John B. Thompson (Cambridge, MA: MIT Press, 1986), 303–4.

39 Pierre Rosanvallon, "Revolutionary Democracy," in Pierre Rosanvallon, *Democracy Past and Future*, ed. Samuel Moyn (New York: Columbia University Press, 2006), 83–84.

40 Quoted in Frank, *Constituent Moments*, 2. The historian Daniel T. Rodgers rightly remarked: "To follow the career of the term The People is to watch men invest a word with extraordinary meaning and then, losing hold of it to other claimants, scuttle from the consequences." Quoted in ibid., 3.

41 Quoted in Reinhart Koselleck, "Volk, Nation, Nationalismus, Masse," in *Geschichtliche Grundbegriffe*, vol. 7, eds. Otto Brunner, Werner Conze, and Reinhart Koselleck (Stuttgart: Klett-Cotta, 1992), 141–431; here 148. As Koselleck put it drily, "Bismarck formulated a form of ideology critique which he was able immediately to deduce from the concept of the people."

42 Sheldon Wolin, "Transgression, Equality, Voice," in Josiah Ober and Charles Hedrick (eds.), *Demokratia: A Conversation on Democracies, Ancient and Modern* (Princeton, NJ: Princeton University Press, 1996), 63–90; here 80.

43 Rosanvallon, "Revolutionary Democracy," 91.

44 Think of the difference between first-wave and second-wave feminism.

45 "Mir geht es um Respekt," in *Die tageszeitung*, September 7, 2013, http://www.taz.de/!5059703, accessed January 2016.

46 For a very illuminating comparison between the cases of Hungary and Egypt, see Gábor Halmai, "Guys with Guns versus Guys with Reports: Egyptian and Hungarian Comparisons," *Verfassungsblog*, July 15, 2013, http://www.verfassungsblog.de/de/egypt-hungary-halmai-constitution-coup, accessed November 13, 2013.

47 Something similar is true of Ukraine, once the Maidan protests became a contest of identitarian claims about what Ukraine really is. I am grateful to Balázs Trencsényi for discussions in this context.

Chapter 3

1 Christopher H. Achen and Larry M. Bartels, *Democracy for Realists* (Princeton, NJ: Princeton University Press, 2016).

2 Josiah Ober, "The Original Meaning of Democracy," in *Constellations*, vol. 15 (2008), 3–9. I don't need to reiterate the usual points about the exclusion of women, slaves, and metics.

3 Peter Mair, *Ruling the Void: The Hollowing of Western Democracy* (New York: Verso, 2013).

4 Cristóbal Rovira Kaltwasser, "The Responses of Populism to Dahl's Democratic Dilemmas," in *Political Studies*, vol. 62 (2014), 470–87.

5 Paulina Ochoa Espejo, *The Time of Popular Sovereignty: Process and the Democratic State* (University Park: Penn State University Press, 2011).

6 See, for instance, Robert B. Talisse, "Does Value Pluralism Entail Liberalism?," in *Journal of Moral Philosophy*, vol. 7 (2010), 302–20.

7 I leave aside here the specifics of Rawls's theory of public reason with its restriction of having to recognize a reasonable pluralism. John Rawls, "The Idea of Public Reason Revisited," in *The Law of Peoples* (Cambridge, MA: Harvard University Press, 1999), 129–80.

8 Quoted in Michael Kazin, *The Populist Persuasion: An American History* (Ithaca: Cornell University Press, 1998), 233.

9 Kazin, *Populist Persuasion*, 241.

10 John Keane, *The Life and Death of Democracy* (New York: Norton, 2009), 277.

11 The book by Akhil Reed Amar, *America's Constitution: A Biography* (New York: Random House, 2006), stresses these popular elements in particular.

12 According to Tim Houwen, "populistic" was coined in 1896 in an article in *The Nation* magazine. See Tim Houwen, "The Non-European Roots of the Concept of Populism" (working paper no. 120, Sussex European Institute, 2011).

13 Keane, *Life and Death*, 340.

14 Quoted in Margaret Canovan, *Populism* (New York: Harcourt Brace Jovanovich, 1981), 33.

15 Ibid., 51, 52.

16 Richard Hofstadter, *The Paranoid Style in American Politics* (New York: Vintage, 2008).

17 Quoted in Kazin, *Populist Persuasion*, 10.

18 Charles Postel, *The Populist Vision* (New York: Oxford University Press, 2007).

19 The book by Bruce Ackerman, *We the People: Foundations* (Cambridge, MA: Harvard University Press, 1993), speaks of a failed constitutional moment (see pages 83–84).

20 C. Vann Woodward, "The Populist Heritage and the Intellectual," in *The American Scholar*, vol. 29 (1959–60), 55.

21 Pippa Norris, "It's Not Just Trump," *Washington Post*, March 11, 2016, https://www.washingtonpost.com/news/monkey-cage/wp/2016/03/11/its-not-just-trump-authoritarian-populism-is-rising-across-the-west-heres-why, accessed April 22, 2016.

22 Martin Gilens, *Affluence and Influence: Economic Inequality and Political Power in America* (Princeton, NJ: Princeton University Press, 2014).

23 Hanspeter Kriesi, Edgar Grande, Romain Lachat, Martin Dolezal, Simon Bornschier, and Timotheos Frey, "Globalization and the Transformation of the National Political Space: Six European Countries Compared," in *European Journal of Political Research*, vol. 45 (2006), 921–56.

24 I have made this argument at greater length in *Contesting Democracy: Political Ideas in Twentieth-Century Europe* (London: Yale University Press, 2011).

25 One might add that dignity—and not freedom—is the master value of postwar constitutions.

26 One might ask in what way, then, "constrained democracy" differs from "guided" or "defective" democracy. The answer is that in the former, genuine changes in who holds power is possible and all constraints are ultimately justified with regard to strengthening democracy. In the latter, no real change is allowed.

27 Nadia Urbinati, "Zwischen allgemeiner Anerkennung und Misstrauen," in *Transit: Europäische Revue*, no. 44 (2013).

28 Chris Bickerton and Carlo Invernizzi, "Populism and Technocracy: Opposites or Complements?," in *Critical Review of International Social and Political Philosophy* (2015), http://www.tandfonline.com/doi/abs/10.1080/13698230.2014.995504, accessed April 28, 2016.

29 See, for instance, Catherine Fieschi, "A Plague on Both Your Populisms!," *Open Democracy*, April 19, 2012, http://www.opendemocracy.net/catherine-fieschi/plague-on-both-your-populisms, accessed March 13, 2014.

30 Wolfgang Streeck, *Gekaufte Zeit* (Berlin: Suhrkamp, 2013).

Acknowledgments

I am grateful to the Institute of Human Sciences (Institut
für die Wissenschaften vom Menschen; IWM) in Vienna
for the invitation to deliver the IWM Lectures in November 2013, on which this book is based. Klaus Nellen and
his colleagues proved wonderful hosts, and I benefited
greatly from discussions with them and the audience during those rainy fall evenings. Another stay at the IWM in
the summer of 2014 helped me develop my ideas further.

Thanks also to the members of the Department of
Politics in Princeton as well as the staff at the Center for
Human Values (its director Chuck Beitz in particular),
who enabled me to host a workshop on populism in 2012.

I am grateful to all those who, during that workshop
and after lectures and seminars, talked with me about a
topic that is of increasing concern to many people in
Europe, the United States, and Latin America at the
beginning of the twenty-first century—even if one cannot
always be sure whether one is even talking about the same
thing. (Richard Hofstadter once gave a talk with the telling title "Everyone Is Talking about Populism, but No One

Can Define It"—a statement that seems not implausible today.)

My thinking about democracy and populism, for better or for worse, took shape in conversations with the following friends and colleagues (which is not to say that I could convince them of my theory): Andrew Arato, David Ciepley, Paula Diehl, Zsolt Enyedi, Gábor Halmai, Dick Howard, Carlo Invernizzi Accetti, Turkuler Isiksel, Dan Kelemen, Seongcheol Kim, Alex Kirshner, Mattias Kumm, Cas Mudde, Cristóbal Rovira Kaltwasser, Ivan Krastev, Ralf Michaels, Paulina Ochoa Espejo, Kim Lane Scheppele, and Nadia Urbinati. Special thanks to Cristóbal for an invitation to Santiago and discussions with him and his colleagues at Diego Portales, and also to Balázs Trencsényi for very helpful conversations when completing the book in April 2016. I am also grateful to Koen Vossen and René Cuperus for information about Dutch politics.

This book draws on the following publications: "Populismus: Theorie und Praxis" (*Merkur*, vol. 69, 2015), "Parsing Populism: Who Is and Who Is Not a Populist These Days?" (*Juncture*, vol. 22, 2015), "'The People Must Be Extracted from within the People': Reflections on Populism" (*Constellations*, vol. 21, 2014), "Anläufe zu einer politischen Theorie des Populismus" (*Transit*, no. 44, 2013), "Towards a Political Theory of Populism" (*Notizie di Politeia*, no. 107, 2012), as well as a number of articles in *Dissent, The New York Review of Books Daily, The Guardian, Le Monde, Die Zeit, Süddeutsche Zeitung*, and *Neue Zürcher Zeitung*.

I am grateful to two editors, both for being patient and for being fast when it mattered: Heinrich Geiselberger, who helped with the German edition of this book, and Damon Linker, who proved an enthusiastic supporter of the American one.

Finally, I am indebted to my family. Special thanks to Heidrun Müller, who helped in various ways when I was completing the book.

This essay is dedicated to my children, who are experiencing their first presidential election campaign consciously and for whom various democratic vistas are wide open. I cannot aspire to be like Whitman, but I can perhaps pay homage by humbly copying the dedication to "him or her within whose thought rages the battle, advancing, retreating, between Democracy's convictions, aspirations, and the People's crudeness, vice, caprices."